Wish You A
GOODE JOURNEY

Living Life With Eyes And Heart Wide Open

MARCY HEATH ROBITAILLE

PRESS

Wish You A GOODE JOURNEY
Living Life With Eyes And Heart Wide Open
by Marcy Heath Robitaille

Printed in the United States of America.

ISBN 9781498464680

www.xulonpress.com

Contents

Dedication

This book is dedicated to those who have been blessed with the gift of a child; whose child has been called back home, seemingly before their time. My hope for you is that you discover the beauty unfolding and cherish the treasures that can be found along your way.

My prayer is this:

> *And may you have the power to understand, as all God's people should, how wide, how long, how high, and how deep his love is. Ephesians 3:18*

Acknowledgments

With heartfelt thanks:

First and foremost to my God and savior Jesus Christ who has carried me most of the way in this at times, unbearable journey, until I saw the pattern of my own footprints in the sand, recognizing His plan for my life.

To my beautiful daughter Makenzie Mia Goode, who created such a lovely legacy for all who knew her; who saved six, and countless other lives by her selfless act of organ donation, and created an amazing story to be shared. You, Kenzie, are my bright shining light, joy and inspiration. You have always been my biggest cheerleader, my encourager. You are my hero and my BFF.

To Pastor/Author Rick Blaisdell, (One Life to Give) my very own personal book angel who was gifted to me to show me how and to encourage me to get this job done. Rick, I consider you a blessing and your help was immeasurable in the editing and formatting of my manuscript. God is GREAT!

To my son Sean, who at most times, was overshadowed by this, our tragedy. I want you to know Sean, you are the best. I love you to the moon and back. You are my BFF.

To my husband Robert, who gave me his love, patience, and protection when I was so fragile. Thank you for understanding that I needed to fly when I had the wings to try it.

To my sister, Sherry and brother in- law David, and my extended family: thank you for your understanding, help and support.

To Kenzie's BFFs (you know who you are), and to my earth angels (you know who you are), thank you for being there for me to lift me up, encourage me, and share this walk with me. I feel so blessed to know you.

Endorsements

Faith Turns Tragedy into Triumph

Wish You a Goode Journey is a very compelling and heart-gripping story of one family's victory over the grief and sorrow of losing a teenage child. This book will be a Godsend to many who find it difficult to find the courage and hope in moving forward after such an experience.

As a pastor, I strongly recommend this book and I will have extra copies in my office as an invaluable tool to help others through the grieving process, and to see them receive their healing from a broken heart. If you're hurting, or know someone who is, don't pass this one up!

Pastor/Author Rick Blaisdell-
One Life to Give

Bringing Light to the World through the Gift of Life

Wish You a Goode Journey is a wonderful testament to love and hope. As the attending physician caring for a teenage girl following her tragic accident, the impact of her life can be difficult to understand, as it is hard to imagine the lives she left behind, following our fateful meeting. The anguish and pain of those few days in the hospital and the ultimate decision to donate her organs remain very real, but this story helps one see how the journey changed course, but continues onward on the path of healing.

This story has been eloquently written by her mom, sharing inspiration that involves family, friends, and donor recipients alike to create a good (e) journey. I am quite inspired, honored, and so incredibly grateful for the ongoing ministry for organ donation and to see how Makenzie's life continues to touch so many. She continues to bring light to the world through her amazing story.

I already know people with whom I will share this story.

Scot T. Bateman, MD
Professor of Pediatrics and Anesthesiology
Vice Chair, Department of Pediatrics
Division Chief, Pediatric Critical Care
University of Massachusetts Medical School
UMass Memorial Children's Medical Center

Hope for Your Goode Journey

Wish You a Goode Journey is a heartfelt story about the tragic death of a teenage girl and how the God of the Universe picked up the shattered pieces of her mom's broken heart and turned them into a marvelous masterpiece for his glory. Living Life with Eyes and Heart Wide Open, Marcy looks to God to give her glimpses of her precious daughter everywhere she goes. He is faithful. The pages of this book resonate with His heart of love, joy, peace and hope in the midst of unthinkable circumstances. The stories of patience in suffering, kindness in adversity, and goodness through hardship will simply melt your heart giving you renewed or new found faith in the Father who created you, loves you, and will give you hope through His son for your own good journey.

Beth Rudy, Author/Speaker, Prayer Pal

God Works All Things for Good

This is a beautifully shared journey of tragedy, loss and grief that transforms into the ultimate gift, the giving of self and a most amazing ripple. It is a true love story, the love of a parent and love of the Lord.

Wherever you are in life, "Wish you a Goode Journey" will have you riveted as you enjoy the robust and enchanting way that Makenzie Goode lived her life, and you will be inspired by her to live your life to the fullest every day. Throughout this journey *Romans 8:28* comes to mind.

And we know that all things work together for good(e) to those who love God, to those who are the called according to His purpose

Renee Olson
Chief Leadership Officer
Nerium International

About the Book

After losing our 17 year old daughter Makenzie Mia Goode in a tragic accident, I feel compelled to share her story. Although initially consumed in grief with her unexpected departure, I have since found joy and healing as the additional chapter to her life unfolds. Makenzie saved six lives through her organ donation and it has been a blessing to get to know these people and hear their stories.

Kenzie continues to show us her fun-loving spirit as little gems are discovered in the treasure hunt of my life. The first being a tiny slip of paper from her collection of saved Chinese cookie fortunes pasted to her mirror. It inspired me with these words: Wish You a Good Journey. Makenzie's last name is Goode and so this was a pivotal moment for me in flipping my emotions. A quest to find joy and happiness has been first and foremost in honoring her memory.

This book is filled with surprising signs "God winks" from above as God offers hope and joy in these "AHA" treasure finds. Come along on my Goode journey by reading about Makenzie and her amazing gifts.

About the Author

Author Marcy Heath Robitaille

Marcy Heath Robitaille is a heart-baring, faith sharing Mom and author who shares her journey of grief, hope and healing in her new book, Wish You a Goode Journey— Living Life with Eyes and Heart Wide Open. After losing her 17 year-old daughter Kenzie in a tragic accident, she recounts the story of her sudden loss—from the depths of depression to soaring new heights, finding joy and surprising treasures along the way. Her book is for anyone who wants inspiration to follow her path and con- nect with the power of God.

Born and raised in New England, Marcy is creating her ripple with her charity work for her daughter's memorial scholarship fund and is a volun- teer with the New England Organ Bank and Donate Life. In supporting mis- sions, she sponsors two children in Kenya and Haiti through Compassion International and Love in Motion to bring hope through these ministries. In addition, Marcy is also a contributor to As Our Own, an organization focused on rescue, aftercare and prevention of children involved in human trafficking.

Marcy is an outdoor enthusiast who enjoys kayaking, bicycling and hiking, and lives simply and quietly in her country home in western Massachusetts with her husband Bob and two Cairn Terriers, Grace and Lily. Not a day goes by that she isn't reminded of Kenzie through (what she refers to as) Godwinks, subtle messages from above.

Introduction

F ather, shine your light in the corners of my soul that your words through this book will be a beacon of hope in this sad world.

Today is the day that I begin our story. When I awoke to my daily inspirational message on my cell phone, this is what it said:

<u>**WRITER :**</u>

> *I will put My law in their minds, and write it on their hearts. Jeremiah 31:33b*

I believe that this was God saying to me: time to get busy. Here is the story of my daughter's gifts and this incredible journey.

Foreword

Reading the Bible in a year was one of the goals that our pastor had set for our congregation each year; only this year "2010" was different. Pastor Garth decided to read it with us as a church creating his sermons around the text based on the chronological Bible that we were all reading. We started in the Old Testament which was slow and difficult reading. Have you ever tried to read the Old Testament and not get distracted by all of the many names that are included to "help" us connect the dots for a "better understanding" of the characters, and who they are related to, in the chapter that is unfolding? Sort of like the sentence that I just attempted to unravel. Anyhow, it was just the beginning of reading the Bible in a year, January 2010, and we were reading passages from the book of Genesis, precisely Chapter 22, which explains how God tested Abraham's faith.

Now it came to pass after these things that God tested Abraham, and said to him, "Abraham". And he said,"Here I am".

Then He said, "Take now your son, your only son Isaac, whom you love, and go to the land of Moriah, and offer him there as a burnt offering on one of the mountains of which I shall tell you".

So Abraham rose early in the morning and saddled his donkey, and took two of his young men with him, and Isaac his son; and he split the wood for the burnt offering, and arose and went to the place of which God had told him. ⁴ Then on the third day Abraham lifted his eyes and saw the place afar off. And Abraham said to his young men, "Stay here with the donkey; the lad and I will go yonder and worship, and we will come back to you".

So Abraham took the wood of the burnt offering and laid it on Isaac his son; and he took the fire in his hand, and a knife, and the two of them went together. But Isaac spoke to Abraham his father and said, "My father"!

And he said, "Here I am, my son".

Then he said, "Look, the fire and the wood, but where is the lamb for a burnt offering"?

And Abraham said, "My son, God will provide for Himself the lamb for a burnt offering". So the two of them went together.

Then they came to the place of which God had told him. And Abraham built an altar there and placed the wood in order; and he bound Isaac his son and laid him on the altar, upon the wood. And Abraham stretched out his hand and took the knife to slay his son.

But the Angel of the LORD called to him from heaven and said, "Abraham, Abraham"!

So he said, "Here I am".

And He said, "Do not lay your hand on the lad, or do anything to him; for now I know that you fear God, since you have not withheld your son, your only son, from Me".

Then Abraham lifted his eyes and looked, and there behind him was a ram caught in a thicket by its horns. So Abraham went and took the ram, and offered it up for a burnt offering instead of his son. And Abraham called the name of the place, The-LORD-Will-Provide, as it is said to this day, "In the Mount of the LORD it shall be provided".

Then the Angel of the LORD called to Abraham a second time out of heaven, and said, "By Myself I have sworn, says the LORD, because you have done this thing, and have not withheld your son, your only son, blessing I will bless you, and multiplying I will multiply your descendants as the stars of the heaven and as the sand which is on the seashore; and your descendants shall possess the gate of their enemies. In your seed all the nations of the earth shall be blessed, because you have obeyed My voice". Genesis 22:1-18.

I read this chapter one morning as I sat in my living room attempting to get through our daily required reading. I pondered the very thought of a loving parent exhibiting this much faith in God, our father and creator, and to actually be willing to sacrifice his only treasured son, Isaac, to obey God. I understood that this was a story and that our loving Father would never ask this of us, but that this was a mere illustration of how God wants to be first and foremost in our lives. I thought about my own faith and wondered if I truly loved God more than my own children who were my treasures in life, God given, of course. I decided that my faith was rock solid and that, NO, I did not love my children more than God, my creator. Little did I know that my faith was about to be tested.

Chapter One

Jesus, Take my Hand!

It was the morning of January 29th, 2010. As any early morning, I woke up and started the coffee and yelled to Makenzie that it was time to get up and off to school. As I was in the kitchen, and looked out the window, I saw a beautiful red fox running through the field across the road. I yelled to Kenz to look out her window to see the fox but, she kept saying, "Where mom, I don't see it". And then it was gone. The morning routine was changed up a bit as my husband Bob was up north at an ice fishing derby leaving me to tend to our outdoor wood burning furnace. I decided to jump in the shower before going outside to stoke the stove, and did not get a chance to visit with my daughter before she left for school. Usually, I would sip my coffee in the living room and chat a bit with her as she got ready and talked about her plans for the day. She would toss the ball for our little dog Gracie a few times, as she was rushing to get ready. Because on this morning, I had decided to take my shower, I never got to chat with Kenz, nor for that matter, even say goodbye. When I came out of the bathroom she had already left for school.

The phone rang a little later and it was the next door neighbor from where I grew up as a child. She was calling to ask me to get in touch with my son Sean who was now living next to her in my dad's house. Sean had come home from a late shift at work and parked his car in their driveway because of the ice on my dad's steep driveway. She needed to get out that morning, so I told her to stay put, and I would come over and get my son up as he was unreachable because his cell phone was shut off. During the time that I was driving over to wake my son up, my daughter was in a terrible accident just moments from our house. She was driving the long way to school as she was told, to avoid an icy commute over the mountain. It was a cold January morning and the winds had blown the snow from the cornfields, in places on the road. As Makenzie approached this incline and bend in the road, she met snow and ice which threw her into a skid and landed her against a lonely fire hydrant on that road. She hit her head and was unconscious. She had suffered a major head injury. It just seems so unfathomable that she wouldn't have just spun her way out into the huge cornfields that were on both sides of that country road. The fact that she hit the only fire hydrant just seemed confusing and incomprehendable.

When I returned from waking my son up, there was a message from the police department asking me to call them. As I did, they proceeded to give me the details of Kenzie's accident although I truly didn't want to hear them. I remember I just kept repeating, "But how is my daughter, tell me how is my daughter"? Eventually the person on the other end explained that she had been airlifted to the University of MA Medical Center and was unconscious. I grabbed my coat and headed back to wake my son up for the second time to have him drive me to the hospital. It was an extremely long ride.

When we arrived at the hospital, they ushered us into a conference room where an entire medical team was waiting for us. I knew it must be bad and that they were going to attempt to prepare me before I went to my daughter's bedside. It was explained that Makenzie had suffered a severe head injury and that her condition was grave. I hated that word, but I liked the doctor, Dr. Bateman, who is the Division Chief of Pediatric Critical Care, of the hospital. After filling us in, they allowed us into her room. They warned us that we needed to be sensitive to what we said in her presence because they were not sure just how much she could hear or comprehend. To see my sweet daughter lying in that bed, she looked so innocent, so small, and so young. By all appearances she looked beautiful. There were no outward physical injuries apparent, although they did tell me she had fractured her leg. I remember talking too much , cheering her on, telling her to be that defensive soccer player that we all knew and loved; explaining that this was the soccer game of her life, and that she needed to go for the goal. The goal I had in mind, of course, was my own selfish desire to keep her here with us in this life. In retrospect, I now can believe that she listened to me and truly did make that goal. I love you Kenzie—good for you!!

There were so many staff members in and out of her room and of course we had our family rallying around her. The nurse who was assigned to Kenzie in the Pediatric ICU was someone who I had met that previous summer up at our camp. We had become friends as our husbands had a love for fishing. I did not realize she was a nurse and found it comforting that she was the assigned nurse for our daughter in those first critical hours. Divine appointment, I believe. I made the decision to have the school called and to make the request that students and friends refrain from coming to the hospital. I felt that knowing my daughter, she would have wanted that privacy. I also thought of these innocent kids and did not want to mar their fond memories of my daughter by seeing her so lifeless. There were few exceptions made, but a few of her closest friends were allowed to come see her with the hopes that they would have just the right words to help her.

Bob and I visited the chapel to pray for a miracle. I remember walking up to the big Bible that was sitting there, and hoping that there might be just the right verse to give me insight and wisdom, but I honestly can't remember what I read. I do remember praying and praying out loud and then suggesting to Bob that we sit quiet to get a sense of what God might have to say. I concentrated on the quiet and truly felt God speaking to me through the Holy Spirit in a very authoritative tone. I felt the words, "I AM IN CONTROL". Briefly afterwards, my family came to find us there sitting in the chapel. We were told that the doctor sent for us to get back to my daughter's room as her blood pressure was very high and they were working on her.

When I got there, Dr. Bateman was directing his staff to save our daughter's life with instructions on increasing this and decreasing that, and monitoring all the machines in full understanding of how she was fighting for her life. It took about ten minutes as we watched and waited. He then called us into that same conference room and explained that they were successful in saving her this time, but what did we want him to do the next time. He felt certain that she was not in a place to rally. Although he was certainly not giving up on her, he just wanted us to know that our daughter would probably in the very best case scenario, never walk, talk, eat, or live life as we knew her too, again. I remember sensing peace as I answered him. I explained to him our visit to the chapel and about God's voice in my heart. I also mentioned what a friend had once said to me about our children, and how they are not our own but on loan from God. The doctor's eyes filled with tears and he said to me, "Your faith is beautiful".

What I realize now, is that God was in control and taking care of matters for me. I need to say here that what I am sharing is my version of how I remember everything. Of course, Kenzie's dad and brother, her aunt and uncle were there with us too and probably have intricate memories of their own. I know her dad was in shock and her brother was not fully understanding, nor in agreement of the seriousness of Makenzie's condition. We decided to give it time as the doctors offered a couple of additional tests to confirm her prognosis.

That same evening of Makenzie's accident, the nurses offered Bob and me a room at the end of the hospital hallway to try and rest. I decided to go lie down and remember lying there shivering. I was freezing. Bob covered me with blankets and more blankets and held me as I shook. I just could not stop feeling ice cold. I gave up on the idea of rest or sleep and went back to her room, only to find that they had packed my daughter in ice because she had spiked a fever. It makes me appreciate how much she and I were connected. I always tell people that my daughter was attached at the hip. We were so very close. She was my best friend and the one with whom I would trust my life. I used to tell her that we were BFF's and she would promptly tell me, as any teenage daughter would, that we were not. I smile, because I know the truth.

Following the testing the next morning, the head of the Pediatric Neurology Department came and found Bob and I to share the test results. I saw the blank look in her eyes; almost like she had to detach herself and speak in automation as she explained the grim details. Her eyes showed no emotion as she told me she was very sorry. I stood there numb and helpless. As a mom, you always feel like you can fix pretty much everything for your kids and always want to. What a feeling of total helplessness as I realized that we were about to be faced with the biggest challenge ever facing a parent. Even though she was on life-support with her life hanging in the balance, we still were faced with letting her go. Myriads of thoughts raced through my mind concerning this decision. How was I going to explain to the waiting room filled with Kenzie's friends, what was happening?

As the ICU Director and medical team sat around the table in that frequented conference room and explained to her daddy, her brother, her aunt and uncle, her step-dad and myself, as well as our two pastors, what was not going on in Kenzie's head and her devastating prognosis, I knew that I had to have a duplicate meeting with Kenzie's friends to include, Matt, Kayla, Danielle, Sasha, Wanda and Maryanne. I requested this of Dr. Bateman, and he concurred. I remember the sweet sentiment of the nurse there who said to me, "Oh my, so much compassion. You don't have to do this". But I knew we did. Kenzie's friends had to be part of this major decision. They needed to know that there was no hope here in this world for Kenzie any longer.

After the meeting, it was decided that her friends would go into her room in pairs to say goodbye. Benny, Kenzie's dad, asked me if we could go in together as we brought her into this world and it would be nice to have a closing talk with her as her parents. This was so painful. As we poured out our hearts to her, I noticed two tears falling down her cheeks from her eyes.

Dr. Bateman approached me, as I deep down knew it was coming, to ask if we would consider organ donation from our daughter. I knew in my heart this was the right option but, we sat as a family for a very long time discussing what we thought would be her wishes. Kenzie was a compassionate and giving person however, she was also a teenager, and we were torn with what we thought she would want us to do. Finally, the decision was made and I sat with the representative from New England Organ Bank to answer the long medical history questions and signing of all the legal documents. Benny, Kenzie's dad, could not stay. His, and Sean's hardest decision was saying goodbye, and then leaving her in that hospital bed alone on life-support while they prepared her body for transplantation. I explained to Sean in the best way that I could, that Kenzie was not with us any longer. Her spirit had already left her body and was seeing amazing things that we could not even fathom. We had to say goodbye. As a family, we stood around her hospital bed as they took her off from the life-support to be sure that she could not breathe on her own. They gave her ten minutes to breathe on her own. That was the fastest ten minutes I have ever endured. The room was full of medical staff and to me this was disheartening but, I feel like the staff had a bond with us and was cheering her on. The last words that I spoke to my sweet daughter while she was alive were, "Kenz, Take Jesus's hand".

January 29, 2010 (Friday)–by Fran P. Another Perspective

I woke up and got ready for school, like any other ordinary day. First period bell rang and lucky enough I had gym class with a handful of my close friends. As we rounded up everyone to walk together to class, there was one of us missing, our girl Kenz. Switching into gym clothes and walking into the gymnasium as Mr. Englehardt takes attendance, he announces, "Makenzie Goode... Guys where's Goode"? As we were talking amongst ourselves, one of us said "not here" as the rest of us agreed she's probably playing hooky, having herself a 3-day weekend.

After first period ended, we carried on with day, as if nothing was wrong. We just needed to get by until 2:27pm when the final period was over, and we had the weekend to look forward to. I was sitting in English class, which happened to be the second to the last period of the day. We were working on group projects or group work, when my two friends Wade and Matt came into the room with news. "Guys we just overheard teachers in the hallway saying Kenzie got into a car accident on the way to school this morning". We thought, no way, that's not possible. With the little service we received on our cell phones, we made calls and text messages to her to see if she would respond, but nothing.

As the bell rang when class was over, a voice came on the loudspeaker saying, "All Seniors report to the auditorium for a mandatory meeting now"! The rumor was true as they announced to all of us that our class-mate Makenzie Goode was in a bad car accident this morning on her way to school and was taken by Life Flight to the hospital. It seemed as if everyone in that room became teary eyed wondering what was going on, how is she, how did it happen?

The final bell rang at 2:27pm and I found myself in the lobby with others trying to figure out whether to go see her at the hospital. Did we just hang out and wait to hear news from someone there? As long as we were all together that is what mattered and we had to get through this awful time. A few minutes later, I found myself with one or two others sitting on the lobby bench in confusion, anger, and sadness, when two of my friends Jordan and Mary, came down from the guidance office. They pulled me aside saying, "We have to tell you something". As I walked into the guidance office door to the direct office of my counselor Ms. Bannister where she, Jordan, Mary, and my other friend Adria were standing, she told me something that emotionally shattered me. "We wanted to let you know we got an update on Kenz's condition and she has little to no brain activity." I couldn't make words other than shouting, "NO"! I turned to walk out of the office as I reached the hallway, I collapsed into the arms of Adria, crying, and hyperventilating. Behind me I heard the voice of my teacher Ms. Brown trying to give comfort, but it seemed with news like that there was nothing that could comfort me.

As the rest of the day carried on, it was the waiting game. Waiting to hear any update, hoping that it was positive, but it all came down to the next day when finding out that the life of my beloved best friend Makenzie Goode, was taken. And that is a day of events I'll never forget.

January 29, 2010 (Friday)–by Alyssa H. Another Perspective

I also remember the day of the accident, we had first block together and I had been wondering where she was. Later in the class, one of the teachers at the school came in. A lot of the day is a blur, but I remember being pulled out of class, and told what had happened. I remember having to hold a meeting with the soccer team in the auditorium, and our coach Socksy came to talk to us, as well. I don't think anyone talked. I don't think anyone said anything, we just sat there. And then we played a game of pick up soccer in the gym together, again without much being said. At that point, I just assumed Kenz would be okay. That weekend I covered her shifts at the nursing home, (we worked together in the dietary dept. at a local nursing home), and Sunday I came home and found out that Kenz wasn't okay. I was in sort of a fight or flight mode emotionally, so I started planning. Kenzie deserved something as she had touched so many people's lives and we needed to come together, as Kenzie would have wanted, so I planned a candlelight vigil. I don't remember how many people came, but I know it was hundreds. Kenzie touched the lives of hundreds of people, in a positive way. Losing one of my best friends has been one of the hardest things. But I am so grateful to have known such an amazing person, and I believe I am better to have known her. She was a leading example of what it is to live like there's no tomorrow, to enjoy things to the fullest, and to not care what anyone thinks of you. I think about Kenz in everything I do and I miss her every day. Life is Goode, I love and miss you BTF.

Candlelight Vigil

Sunday evening a candle light vigil was held at the school. As you can imagine, I was unable to attend. I was a mess. I wish to thank Alyssa H. and others for having the strength, and genuine love for our daughter to make this happen. The newspaper reported that a crowd of over 300 huddled in the cold at the school that Sunday evening. Several people spoke including Matt, Makenzie's boyfriend. He fought back tears as he explained that her smile is what he is going to miss the most. He told them that she had become his best friend as they had known each other since the ninth grade. Makenzie's brother, Sean attended and also spoke. He told the crowd that she would want us to keep going. He also said: "She's with us. She's not gone; talk to her, pray to her".

In an article from the Greenfield Recorder newspaper, Arn Albertini reported this:

Pioneer Community in mourning – 2/01/2010
NORTHFIELD

Makenzie Goode will be remembered for her smile, sense of humor and the joy she brought all who met her.

Goode, 17, of Warwick, died Saturday at University of Massachusetts Memorial Healthcare Center in Worcester after being involved in a car crash on Friday morning in Winchester, NH.

Goode was a senior at Pioneer, where she had played soccer for six years. She worked at Applewood Nursing Home in Winchester.

"She's amazing", said Sarah Devine. "I think her personality made up 99 percent of our senior class". All students, no matter their social group or class, liked Goode. Devine said. "I don't think I ever had a day go by without hearing a joke from her". Asked what she'll miss most, Devine said, "Her faces."

Junior Alyssa Hill, who played soccer with Goode, said they had a habit of making goofy faces on the soccer field, especially when they were called for playing rough.

Goode liked to drive various places and hold impromptu dance parties, said Hill. "She would just crank up the music and dance in the parking lot." Sometimes that dance site was at the grocery store, other times it was at a local department store and a few times it was at school.

Mandy Oliver-Rowe teaches chorus at Pioneer. She said she didn't have Goode in any classes, but many of her students were good friends with her and she spoke with Goode the day before she died. "She just had the biggest smile that you couldn't forget even if you weren't close to her".

Friends say she was hoping to attend Plymouth State University next fall, where her boyfriend is a freshman.

Candlelight Vigil—Photo by Greenfield Recorder's Peter MacDonald

Friends and family gathered outside Pioneer Valley Regional School Sunday evening for a candlelight vigil in memory of Makenzie Goode, who died Saturday from injuries she sustained in a car accident on Friday. **Peter MacDonald**

The week flew by as we prepared for her services. We decided to wait a week and have the service on a Saturday so that anyone from school could attend. The calling hours were held on that Friday night before and the line was so long that I was told it took approximately two hours to get to the front to our receiving line. I remember entering the church and seeing pictures everywhere of Makenzie. There wasn't any free wall space. I was told that the school allowed the kids to work on picture boards during their school day, throughout the entire week to prepare for this. At the end of the calling hours I remember seeing Kenzie's group of friends standing in the back waiting for me. They were kind of smiling sheepishly when I went back to see what they were doing. I said to them, "Ok, what's up, what are you girls up to"? They laughed and all put their hands in a circle and lifted their sleeves. Each had gotten a tattoo on their wrists that said KENZ, MIA or MMG. I asked them if their parents knew that they had done this and they smiled and one said, "Now, they do". This left such an amazing impression on me. (I told Chelsea the next day that although Mia is Kenzie's middle name, it also is an acronym for Missing in Action).

When we arrived at her funeral, we saw many busses parked in the church parking lot. It was standing room only; in excess of 500 people in attendance; just confirmation of the love so many had for her and our family. The church was adorned with pictures...hundreds of pictures of her...her goofy ways, her spirited self, very uplifting. Some of the smallest details that I recall were a big jar of tootsie rolls at the entrance, (Kenzie's favorite candy), and homemade corn chowder on the buffet table (another favorite), for the reception after. The school chorus performed under the direction of Mandy Oliver and sang with my sister, Sherry. I asked them to sing "Immanuel, Our God is with Us" and they sang it beautifully, along with other selections. I must add here that PVRS was so supportive of us. Losing Makenzie in her senior year was a devastating loss for this small school. Everyone knew her; she was the spirited one. I recall that she and a guy friend, Pat V., were asked to lead the Pep Rally for Homecoming weekend at the school. Of course, who else? After the service, a very funny power-point video was played over and over again with so many videos of Kenzie's antics, including when she dressed in a Hanna Montana wig and strolled through a shopping mall totally committed to being noticed. I feel certain that Kenz was smiling her biggest smile as we celebrated her life.

Another song that was sung seemed perfect for Makenzie's service; it was selected because I hoped that the lyrics would resonate with her young friends.

SUNRISE OF YOUR SMILE by Michael Card
*Reject the worldly lie that says,
That life lies always up ahead,

Let power go before control
becomes a crust around your soul,

Escape the hunger to possess
And soul-diminishing success,

This world is full of narrow lives,
I pray by grace your smile survives.

Chorus- For I would wander weary miles,
Would welcome ridicule, my child,

To simply see the sunrise of your smile,
To see the light behind your eyes,

The happy thought that makes you fly,
Yes, I would wander weary miles,

To simply see the sunrise of your smile.
*Now close your eyes so you can see,

Your own unfinished memories,
Now open them, for time is brief,

And you'll be blessed beyond belief,
Now glance above you at the sky,

There's beauty there to blind the eye,
I ask all this then wait awhile,

To see the dawning of your smile

Chorus-

(License for Use granted by Capitol CMG Publishing)

SEAN

I wanted to write about our son. I honestly can't speak to how he is feeling. He shares little to no thoughts with me about losing his sister; he suffers silently. He just cannot talk about her. Five years have passed and still when I offer to send him a funny video or share something that she said, he merely replies, "Not yet, mom", and "but keep it safe, save it".

He and his sister were very close. Raising them in a very secluded little town in the woods has its merits such as fresh air and safety. However, it also lends itself to a bit of loneliness. When Makenzie's big brother moved out, she was very much an only child here. Lots of driving ensued to get her to friends where she would have "something to do". She rarely wanted friends to come here as there was nothing to do. Our little town consists of a church and a library. That's it. No stores, not even a red-light.

Kenzie with her brother Sean and me

After Makenzie had her accident, my son was there with me pleading with me not to let her go. He begged me to let him take care of her forever. Of course his heart was so right, but we knew that Makenzie would not have wanted to live the remainder of her life fully incapacitated. We were told after several tests that there was no hope. On the evening of her accident, Sean left the hospital to drive to the scene of her accident to pick up everything left behind; scraps of metal and glass. He did not want any negative reminders there. He surprised me by actually rescuing the wooden fence post with the barbed wire that she had knocked over. He asked me later on if we could do something special with it, like plant it in a flower garden. So, thanks to my husband Bob, it is front and center of our flower garden at the house with a big purple butterfly sitting on it. Another one of Sean's ideas really surprised me. On what would have been Makenzie's 18th birthday, just three and a half months after her death, Sean told me that he had planned on going to the church and requesting permission to ring the church bell in the belfry 18 times to celebrate his sister's life. I was amazed that he thought of that.

It was at her brother's request that we asked that no one leave any crosses, flowers, notes, or anything at the accident scene. We actually had someone call the high school to relay this to the students while we were at the hospital. For me, as her mom, I felt like it would be very difficult to drive by two or more times per day and also worried about how horrible it would make us feel when the activity eventually stopped. For Sean, however, he worried that this "shrine", as you will, might be littered on and he said that he would be very upset to find any random litter next to a cross that was put there to honor his sister's life. He is very thoughtful and loves his little sister to the very core of his being.

Our garden with the recovered fencepost

I wrote my thoughts down in a journal quite consistently in the beginning. I was fearful that I might forget things and wanted to be able to come back to my thoughts and memories, if I needed. One of my journal entries I thought that I would share here:

33

I wonder what God might place on my heart this eve. And then, I think of this. I have this framed picture of a sunset hanging at my camp. I bought it because the words resonated with me. It is entitled,

A Moment

by: Sharon Poet

I remember a moment, so real.
Love whispered for me to feel.
In that moment, I opened—to let it in.
And forever long for that moment again.

I had a moment like that, an amazing moment when I experienced the love and peace of our Father in heaven like I have never experienced before. His love penetrated my heart and soul. His love enveloped me, and dwelled within me. It was an amazing feeling that I did not want to stop feeling. This is how it all came about. My husband Bob and I had been watching a movie downstairs and Bob placed the movie on pause to take the dog out for a quick walk. I sat in that room and remembered that the very last moments that I spent with my daughter were in that room, sitting on that couch with her. Makenzie had come home from an evening at Matt's and sat down to visit with me for a little while. She started playing a little game with our dog Gracie. Gracie would run at top speed around and around the room and up over our laps and down on the floor and around and around and around. Every time Gracie would come up and across our laps, Kenzie would squeal in delight and that would get Gracie running even faster. We use to call Gracie, Racie Gracie.

Kenzie with Matt and Gracie

At that memory of my last evening with my daughter, I suddenly sank into deep, deep despair. I cried so very hard over missing Kenz. Uncontrollable sobs like I hadn't cried before. I wondered how these sounds could be making their way out of me. It didn't sound like me. That was one of my darkest moments after losing her. As I lay there on the couch sobbing, I experienced that moment. I felt Jesus holding me; rescuing me, loving me with a love that I have never felt before. I did not want it to end.

Through the LORD's mercies we are not consumed, because His compassions fail not. They are new every morning; great is Your faithfulness. "The LORD is my portion" says my soul, "Therefore I hope in Him"! Lamentations 3:22-24

THE PRAYER SHAWL

I am amazed at the power of prayer. I know that there were so many people praying for our family. A couple of months after we lost Kenzie, I decided to go back to church. It wasn't that I didn't want to go to church, I just felt like I didn't want to cry anymore. For me, church can be emotional as well as spiritual. There are so many memories of my children shared in church; sweet memories that I cherish. Sunday school, musical performances, Christmas plays and the annual Santa Lucia event in which Kenzie participated. After church that first time back, I was approached by the assistant pastor's wife and she asked me if I would join her and a few of the ladies back in the pastor's office for a few minutes. All I could think was that these lovely Christian ladies had sweet intentions, but, how would I get through this. But the love of Christian friends is so different. We have a bond that is greater and deeper than mere friendship. We are family; part of God's family.

These beautiful Christian friends had asked me to join them so they could present a gift to me. They had created a beautiful purple prayer shawl. It was explained to me that as the shawl was made, they prayed over it. At the time, they did not know who would be the benefactor. Also pointed out to me was that the stitch that was used forms a cross. Their hope for me was that I would feel Christ's peace from the many prayers that had gone into it. I was awestruck. What a heartfelt gift and it was purple. For months afterwards, each time that I would begin to sink into sadness, I would take the prayer shawl and wrap myself in it. I am truly amazed at the peace that I would feel. Peace, Christ's amazing peace. I think of the Bible verse from John: *Peace I leave with you, My peace I give to you; not as the world gives do I give to you. Let not your heart be troubled, neither let it be afraid. John 14:27.*

Chapter Two

Kenzie's Perfect Day-The Lifeline Letters

"You can't have a perfect day without doing something for someone who'll never be able to repay you". John Wooden, Legendary UCLA Basketball Coach-(Public Quote)

S everal weeks after Kenzie left us, I received my first letter from one of her organ recipients. It was a letter written by his three sons thanking us for her gift of life.

Dear Family,

> *I am sure this letter may be difficult to read, it is difficult to write. Our deepest condolences go out to your family. Please know that not a day goes by that your family is not in our thoughts and prayers. We are writing this letter to say Thank You for the decision to save a life in your time of grief. Somehow the words "Thank You" don't seem big enough for what your family has courageously done for ours. We wanted your family to know how grateful we are; that because you gave us part of your family, we have the opportunity to spend these precious moments with our father, grandfather, husband, brother, and friend. We would not have our father today if not for your family's most precious donation. We are truly saddened by the pain your family has endured. This is*

why every time we look at Dad we remember your loss. Dad is home now and he is spending every waking moment with his loving wife and impish grandkids. They truly love their "Papa" and are enjoying having him back home. Thank you for this second chance at life.

Forever Grateful,
Recipient and Family

It was so great to receive this first letter and I knew I had to write back right away.

The next morning as I was getting dressed, I noticed on my dresser a **Guideposts** magazine that had been sitting there for months unread. On the cover was an article about a mother who lost her daughter similarly and her quest to find the recipient of her daughter's liver. This first letter that I had just received the day before was from the family of the recipient of my daughter's liver. Hmmmm. So, I sat down and wrote a letter to all of Kenzie's recipients and also shared a copy of the **Guidepost's** article with each of them. Here is the letter that I wrote:

April 2010
Dear Recipient and Family,

Thank you for your beautiful letter; for acknowledging the gift we were able to give. As Makenzie's mother, I could not imagine doing anything else as to somehow make this, our horrible tragedy meaningful.

Our daughter, Makenzie, was a beautiful 17 year old girl. She was full of life and love but, mostly compassion. She brought so much joy to the lives she touched; a remarkable young woman who had so much to give. Kenzie was a strong athlete and played soccer since she was in second grade. She earned a spot on the varsity soccer team since only a freshman (she considered this a very big accomplishment) and was also named MVP in her sophomore year. Makenzie had been accepted to attend a University in the fall with her boyfriend and both planned on obtaining their degree to teach physical education and coaching. She was an honor student and worked part-time at a local nursing home where her grandfather was a resident.

Makenzie has left one brother who misses her badly and her daddy who loves her dearly.

I guess I am sharing all this to provide a sense of the individual she was and of how blessed we feel to have had her as our daughter for 17 wonderful years.

I was praying that someone would write to us and you did. Thank you.

We will be attending the graduation on June 4th as her friends insist she will be there and graduating right alongside of them. She was very popular and most of her friends had called her their best friend. I am no exception. I use to tease her that we were BFFs and she would just sigh and roll her eyes and smile. Makenzie always smiled and will be remembered that way.

The morning after I received your letter, I glanced down at my bureau and on it was an old issue of Guideposts with an article that I had never read. Since I felt it was such a "coincidence" that I would find this particular article to read, I am enclosing a copy for you to read as well.

If you would not find it difficult to correspond, I would welcome the opportunity, as to me, in you, our daughter lives on. Thank you for that.

Blessings to you, and your wonderful family,
Sincerely,
Marcy
Kenzie's mom

I have since heard from five of the recipients and have been regularly corresponding with four of them.

The next letter arrived in June 2010. It arrived on my birthday. Michael, who suffered from Cystic Fibrosis his entire life, received Kenzie's lungs.

Dear Marcy and Donor Family,

> *Thank you so very much for your kind letter and sharing with our family information about Makenzie. My husband, son, and I are writing this letter together, as we all have so much to thank you for, and we are so emotionally moved at this time.*

> *We want to first extend our condolences in the loss of your daughter. Many prayers were said for the donor and family. We can't comprehend what you and your family must have gone through, and continue to go through. But we hope that this letter can offer you some comfort and consolation in knowing that your generous "Gift of Life" has given our son a second chance at life.*

> *It is clear from your letter that Makenzie was very loved, very giving and caring towards others, and enjoyed life. After reading about her love of sports and her athletic abilities, it was clear that she was a very strong young woman. Her organ gift to our son was her lungs.*

> *Our son's name is Michael. To give you an idea of the impact Makenzie's organ donation has had on his life, and our family's life, let us now share with you about Michael's experiences.*

> *Michael is a 38 year old man who has lived with Cystic Fibrosis his entire life. Over the past 9 years, his health declined to a point where he struggled to get through each day. He had enjoyed living independently, working, sharing time with friends, playing his drums, mountain biking, and*

spending time with his sister and her husband, but slowly had to give up most of these things.

Over the course of last year, he was dominated by back to back hospitalizations, hours of medical treatments each day, while trying to stay healthy enough to get to transplant in time. He fought hard every day and did not give up.

On January 29th, Michael was admitted to the hospital. As parents, we did not believe that he would come out of the hospital as his condition seemed so critical. Two days later, the morning of January 31st, after 8 long years of waiting on the transplant list, our prayers were answered. We were advised that Michael would begin his preparation for a possible transplant later in the day.

We are a small family of four, but we have a very large support family who immediately offered up prayers and lit a candle for the generous donor (and family) for the "Gift of Life". Prayer lines up and down the East Coast were sharing the news as they had been praying for Michael for a very long time.

Michael's recovery from the double lung transplant has been amazingly fast. We had been told that the lungs were young and that they were good. He progressed through his Surgical ICU stay quickly and was up and walking (with assistance) before he continued his inpatient time in a Transplant (stepdown) Unit.

Michael challenged himself daily in both units by walking laps around the ward and continued to grow stronger through his recovery. By 3½ weeks post-transplant, he was able to come home. He gives thanks every day for the gift he has been given, which has allowed him to restart his life. It is truly the "Gift of Life."

When home, he started immediately into a program of working out which has involved use of the treadmill, but now he enjoys long walks in the out of doors on nice days. He was allowed to start using weights and other exercise equipment which has paid off in regaining his strength and stamina again. Do you suppose he has gotten some support and coaching from a special physical education angel?

While Michael was in the hospital he thought of several things he would like the opportunity to do again. He recently participated in the Great Strides Walk-a-thon to benefit the Cystic Fibrosis Foundation. He completed the 6 mile walk accompanied by his doctor of over 20 years, and one of his favorite nurses, who also participated.

Music was a very important part of Michael's life before he became too weak to play his drums. He is now able to reclaim that joy again.

As you and your family read this letter, we want you to know how precious this gift is, and that your loss is not taken lightly. Michael fought to stay as healthy as he could and to be ready and worthy of the organs when the donor match came through. After reading about Makenzie, and her physical strength, it is no wonder Michael has progressed so well. And yes, through him your daughter lives on.

Our family has been truly blessed. We hope that by sharing with you we have in some way helped you as well.

Thank you for the article you enclosed. We had sincerely hoped that we would have the opportunity to thank the donor family at some point out and appreciate your taking the first step this soon.

In closing, Michael wants you to know that he welcomes future correspondence from your family if you choose to. He is extremely thankful for the gift he has been given, and our thoughts and prayers are with your family.

With Sincere Gratitude,
Michael, Suzanne and Gerard

I received several letters from Michael's mother and also Michael. I am including one of his letters here dated 12/15/2011 (two years post -transplant).

Dear Marcy,

> *Thank you for your last letter. I feel more comfortable the more that I write you! Yes, I play drums with my former bassist Randy for improvised fun. Then I play with my band Vintage Flesh. We are very much a heavy metal/punk band. We like to play at quick tempos, then, slow it right down. I joined an indie rock band too, and my drumming is coming along really well. I always thank Makenzie for that, as I just would not have the lung power to do this otherwise.*

> *That's great that you are writing to three of Makenzie's recipients. We all owe you and your family a great deal. I wish I could have met Makenzie. Her picture on my fridge is a great reminder of how very selfless some people are. That is very good that you are involved with the organ bank. I always am impressed to see someone has signed up as a donor.*

> *Recently, I have met a wonderful woman in my life. She and I had been good friends for 8 years, and I finally worked up the nerve to ask her out. We have been very happy for months now. I have a good feeling Krista and I will be together for the long run. All my friends say we are "disgustingly cute" together! That amuses me greatly!*

> *I feel at a loss for the right words, but I wish to express my gratitude towards Makenzie for donating her lungs to me.*

She saved my life, period. I wish to thank you for all your strength and thanks for writing to me.

Myself, along with my family, wish your family a very Merry Christmas and Happy New Year too..

Take Care,
Michael

P.S. I am doing very well, had my doctor's check-up and things are good!

Larry, who is now in his 70's, and the recipient of Makenzie's heart, had struggled with writing at first, not knowing how to thank us. Larry had suffered from ischemic cardiomyopathy. I had asked him in one of my letters as I have asked each person, if he had noticed any changes in his life whether it is a new-found fondness for a food, or music, or whatever—this is what he wrote: "The biggest change I have noticed is that I have greater feelings for others. You know, like when a heartwarming story is being told, I tend to choke up more. I mean, a lot more. I am an ex-Marine and really never allowed emotion like this before. I am sort of enjoying these new emotions. Maybe the new me is a better person than the old me. I do think that Makenzie is still living within me". He added in another letter, "You're right about small miracles. I believe I am seeing them everywhere. Makenzie's heart has given me new insight into things that I never paid attention to before. I believe, as you do, that God has chosen to give me Makenzie's heart for a reason. I don't know what the reason is, but I pray every night that He gives me the strength and courage to do the task He has for me, and that I do not fail Him".

Next, I received a beautiful card on the anniversary date of Kenzie's death (it had a butterfly on it) from Al and his wife Tina. Al suffered from diabetes, starting with juvenile diabetes as a child. He is the recipient of Makenzie's pancreas. In their card was this letter:

Marcy,

*I wanted to send you this card to let you know we think of
Makenzie often, also of you and your family and how you
must be doing with today being the 1 year—*

*If I could come and give you a hug in person I would, but
the organ bank has their guidelines which I understand that
both families would have to agree to, but please whenever
you are ready or if ever—We would be more than honored
to meet you and your family to thank you personally—*

*My husband received Makenzie's pancreas. He is doing
very well.*

*But I have a question about Makenzie, if you wouldn't
mind answering. Did she eat a lot of peanut butter and
apple slices?? That has become my husband Al's favorite
thing lately to the point that we buy two jars of peanut
butter at a time.*

*I am not even sure if you got my last letter or you will
receive this one.*

*In the letter that you sent last spring you mentioned that you
would like to keep in touch. Well I would also like that, so
if the organ bank has some forms that need to be filled out I
am more than willing to sign them.*

Again, I hope you and the family are well.

Hugs to you and yours,
Tina and Al

We eventually met Al and Tina and their beautiful three daughters, as
we entertained them up at our summer camp for a cookout and campfire.
Al, at one point during their visit, asked me to come sit down next him. He

said to me, "What I am about to share with you is probably going to make you cry". I said with some hesitation, "Well, ok". Al explained to me about how his organ donation process happened. He had gotten the call in the evening and went to the hospital. He explained that he had been chosen as the "alternate" recipient. I guess that means that if for whatever reason, the primary candidate does not meet their criteria the alternate will be the recipient. Al explained that they do not know anything about the person from whom the organ is being gifted. He shared with me that when he was in recovery trying to wake up, he heard a young girl's voice calling for her mom. My thoughts raced as he told me this as I was wondering what did she sound like? Was she in pain? Was she angry or stressed? He explained to me that it was like a confirmatory voice: like "Mom! Mom!" I'm here and look at what we've done! This information would not leave me all day as I worried and worried. In the evening I asked Al to explain again to me what he heard. Tina, Al's wife spoke up and told me that it was only her and Al in the recovery room, (that his mom was not there). She explained just as Al did, and that she actually heard Al calling for mom in the same fashion that he had shared. As if, he was looking for his mother. After that, I remember saying to Al that I believed he received our daughter's organ for a very important reason. He has three beautiful daughters to walk down the aisle at their future weddings. During our visit throughout that day, Gracie, Kenzie's Cairn terrier, stayed close to Al. He took her for several walks and they seemed to just have this connection. Before he left, he offered to take Grace home with him but, well of course, that was not an option for me.

Al and Tina came again to support me when I spoke on National Donor Sabbath at church two years after Kenzie's accident. We have had a nice connection and I consider them special friends. Al has certainly had his share of health challenges including an auto accident following his pancreas transplant. Tina explained that prior to Al's pancreas transplant she had given him her kidney the year before in July, as he had gotten very sick. Now he has two transplanted organs. She also shared that Al had been involved in a car accident after receiving Makenzie's pancreas and his team of doctors were very concerned. They required a CT scan to be certain there was no injury or complications to his internal organs. Al explained to me that when they performed the CT scan, they found three working kidneys!! You see, when they transplanted Tina's kidney, they did not remove Al's diseased kidney, but just left it. Usually the diseased organ will just shrivel up. In Al's case, he received Makenzie's perfect pancreas which worked so well that his bad kidney started working again. He had three working kidney's in him, and two pancreases!! Wow, a whole lot of organs for this wonderful guy.

We have since met several times, and because of this, Kenzie's best gift, we were honored guests at their oldest daughter Monica's wedding in June 2015. What a blessing.

I received a letter from Felicia and her mother Michelle in February 2012. Felicia is the recipient of one of Makenzie's kidneys. The letters were so heartfelt. Michelle wrote the letter addressing Makenzie as Beautiful Angel. It really struck a chord with me since she too, has a daughter that she loves with all her heart. Felicia was twelve when she got so very sick. Here is their letter.

Al walking daughter Monica down the aisle

To my angel's family,

> *I'd like to start by saying I 'm extremely sorry for your loss and to also thank you for giving my daughter the gift of life. I'm sorry this has taken so long. I had given the transplant center a letter over a year ago to send to you, come to find out, unfortunately they hadn't sent it.*

> *I know that it must have been a very difficult decision to make in your time of pain, but you had chosen to help another family, for which I will be forever grateful to you.*

> *I know your loved one is resting peacefully in God's arms. Although we've not met, I consider you a part of my family, and you'll always be in my thoughts and prayers.*

I want you to know that your loved one continues to live through my daughter Felicia and I know others thoughts, prayers, and love are sent your way, my angel's family.

To my angel,

May you always continue to rest peacefully in God's arms, continue to watch over your loved ones.

Sincerely,
Michelle & Felicia

In March 2012 I received this letter from Felicia:

Marcy,

Hello, I am Felicia. I am fourteen years old. I will be fifteen years old on March 8, 2012. I got sick with a rare kidney disease at only 11 years old. Three months before my 12th birthday it was hard as I did not know what was happening, so my mom explained it to me. She said "Felicia honey, you have kidney failure". I cried a lot and I was hospitalized for three and a half weeks. They did all types of testing. Then I started dialysis three days a week: Tuesday, Thursday, and Saturday. It made me really tired and sick. I had a catheter which connected to my heart. There are two ports one red and one was blue. It helped filter the bad blood and give me good blood. Dialysis lasted thirteen months. I was listed for about a month. I got the call January 31st 2010 at 7:21 a.m. My mom was cleaning the house and I was sitting on the couch. My mom's face said it all. She said "go get dressed and pack your bag". I screamed. We got to the hospital so quickly. I didn't go into surgery until 10:00 pm. My mom, nana, cousin, aunt, my dad and stepmother were all there. I want to say thank you for the gift of life. I know I would not be here if it wasn't for my new kidney. I am sorry for your loss and I feel like I have another mom and dad out there.

Thank you. I was happy to get my life back. But it was hard for me to find out someone had to die for me.

THANK YOU MAKENZIE, MAY YOU REST IN PEACE. YOU ARE A PART OF ME.

SINCERELY, FELICIA

We corresponded and soon after exchanged email addresses. The way that communication happens through the Organ Bank is a rather lengthy process. If a recipient writes a letter to the donor family, it first goes to the recipient's organ bank who then forwards it on to the donor family's organ bank. Then a letter is sent to the donor family to see if they would like to receive the letter. In turn, the donor family writes or calls to say they would like to receive the letter, and then it is mailed. It is indeed, quite the production. The communication is also very confidential in that nothing is allowed such as last names, places or anything that might reveal information about the donor or recipient. All pertinent information is protected. Each organ bank reviews every communication to be sure that nothing is revealed that shouldn't be. They actually will black out anything that could be considered compromising, making communication challenging. Once we decided that we each wanted to learn more about the other, we had to contact the Organ Banks and let them know. In turn, legal paperwork was mailed to both recipient and donor families where we were required to "sign off" any recourse for such an exchange taking the Donor Banks out of the loop, so to speak. Michelle, Felicia, and I instantly knew that this had to happen.

My friend Betty went with me to meet Felicia and her mom Michelle, as well as Felicia's siblings. We met at the Boston Aquarium. I remember I approached them standing in front of the Aquarium, they both were crying. I reassured them that there would be no tears on that day; that we would be only sharing happiness. We had a nice visit and had pizza later. Michelle explained to me how very sick her little girl had been. Before she was sick she weighed 120 pounds, but, when she was at her worst, she had gotten down to 55 pounds. She said she put her daughter in a taxi and headed for Children's Hospital. When she got there, she told the doctors that they HAD to figure out what was wrong with her daughter.

I remember throughout the day of our visit we continued to see little reminders. A Life is Good bumper sticker and a Good Times t-shirt. Then, when Betty and I went to get ice cream at the end of the day, I saw graffiti painted on the outside wall facing my table. It said Be Good! Ha ha...my daughter is always looking out for me. Felicia and her mom and I have stayed in touch via social media. I have appreciated watching Felicia grow up over these past several years, from an adolescent into a young woman. I believe that her mom is a good mom. I have watched as Felicia continues to struggle with medical challenges post-transplant and can only imagine how nerve wracking this must be for Michelle. I know she loves her daughter with all her heart.

A note from Felicia -five years later:

> *Hello, my name is Felicia. I'm 18 years old now. I received a kidney transplant. At 11 years old I was diagnosed with a rare kidney disease called Anti GBM, I was terrified. I didn't know if I was going to make it or not. I had a long road ahead of me with countless trips to the emergency room, dialysis three days per week / four hours at a time. There were many hospital stays, so many IVS, blood draws and a good handful of surgeries. There were days that I would lay in bed and think to myself "Is today the day" or "Thank God I made it another day". Having kidney problems is no joke; it's extremely hard to live with. I wasn't a normal 11 year old. I would sleep all the time. I couldn't eat and I was only able to drink a certain amount daily. People ask me if it was difficult. Yes, it was difficult because I wasn't sure if I was going to get better. The only people that stayed by me was my mother and grandmother. They were my biggest supporters and they knew how to make me laugh and smile through this difficult time. Not only did my mother have me to take care of and worry about, but she had a beautiful two year- old at home; a blonde with big beautiful blue eyes and a contagious smile. My little sis didn't understand what was going on as she was too young. All she did was ask my mom, "When will sissy come home?" All my mother could say was*

not today. I lived with this for thirteen and half months, but things were about to change tremendously.

On January 31, 2010 at 7:21 a.m. in the morning, my house phone rang. A number from another state popped up on our caller I.D. At first my mother wasn't going to answer it but something told her to. Thank God she did, as it was my doctor. He told my mother that they had a kidney for me and not to rush to the hospital, but we did. We got to Children's Hospital in Boston where I was about to have the biggest surgery of my life. As a matter of fact, my surgery was ten hours long. I couldn't believe it when it was actually going to happen. It all happened because of a wonderful girl and her amazing and strong mother's decision to save so many people's lives as she did, and I can't thank her enough for my kidney. My favorite quote from a woman who has a special place in my heart is one I think about every day. Her quote is: "Life is Goode".

Felicia heading to her prom

Almost six years later my kidney is working wonderfully. It took me a while to talk about getting a kidney transplant because I felt different but that was because I went through something so life changing and I stayed as positive as I could no matter what was going on. I know there is a part of her in me. I never met my angel physically but I know she's by my side spiritually and helping me when I'm having a difficult time or hitting road blocks in my life. I'm thankful to have her mother in my life, even though I met her only once, she's one of my biggest inspirations. Being a transplant patient changes your outlook on life completely; not only because you take medication for the rest of your life, but because it makes you understand

the value of life and how only one person can change so many
lives in such a positive way that she did. Organ donation
is a beautiful thing and so many lives are saved every year
because of organ donation.

A Heart of Gold

My connection with Larry has been amazing. This sweet man who is blessed with my daughter's heart is a perfect pick. But, ah, God never makes mistakes. Larry explained to me that the heart must be a perfect match. Even the doctors are amazed at how wonderfully he has done with Makenzie's heart and his body has not shown any signs of rejection. Larry was not the first to write to me. In fact, it took him some time to be able to gather his thoughts enough to attempt to write. He was at a loss for words. He even explained in his first letter that he was encouraged by his chaplain to write to us after I had reached out to all of the recipients with my first universal letter. I cannot describe why it was so utterly important that I communicate with the recipient of my daughter's heart but, I guess I will just say that you can only imagine. There was this huge vacancy in my own heart, a void, and I longed to know about the person who received my daughter's heart. It was a missing piece of me that needed to be reconnected.

We were up at our camp that summer when my husband's family all came for the annual seafood fest and family reunion. Melody, his cousin, came in from New York. This was my first time meeting Melody and we hit it off. She is the kind of person who is easy to get to know and has a very sweet, supportive, listening ear. I certainly took advantage of that during the weekend. After I shared so much about my daughter and how she saved so many lives, Melody told me that she had a book for me. Actually, the book had been given to her prior to her coming on this weekend and she did not really understand why the book was given to her. She promptly gave me the book and said that she now understood that the book was intended for me. The book was all about the heart and our connections spiritually. The writer talked about how the heart actually has a mind or soul that speaks out if we intently pay attention and listen. The remainder of our summer, I read the book. One night as I was lying in bed with my husband, I proceeded to tell him about what I was reading as I do quite often. I told him that my heart needed to speak to Makenzie's heart, and to let it know that I really needed to learn more about and communicate with the recipient. I remember Bob telling me that my heart needed to go to sleep. Ha ha.

That summer I spent a lot of time at our camp as it was an escape for me. It felt like a relief not to have to deal with the looks, the sadness, and the hugs from so many well-meaning friends and acquaintances by merely running into them on the street or in the stores back home. My loving friends and family did not realize that as well intentioned as they were, I just did not want to cry anymore; at least not in front of people. I begged off from every imaginable invitation that I received that first year. This included momentous occasions such as big birthdays, graduation cele-brations, and weddings too. I just did not want to have to talk about my daughter. I was lost and did not want to be found. I felt most of the time as if I was on auto pilot and I guess I truly was, as God was in control and I knew it. Bob left me to go back home the following day after I was sharing about the heart book that I was reading. Mid-week during one of his many calls to check on me, he told me that I had received a letter from New England Organ Bank. I immediately told him to open it up and read it. It was my first letter from Larry. I guess my heart finally spoke to her heart. Again, I must say, God is so good.

So here is where I will share Larry's first letter to us. It was evident that he certainly struggled with what to say.

Dear Marcy,

> *This letter is to thank you, Kenzie's dad, and your son for the heart your family so generously gave to me. The reason this letter was so long in coming was because I could not think of any way possible to thank you for saving my life after you suffered such a tragedy in your own lives. I still cannot find the words to express my appreciation.*

> *I read your description of Makenzie and what a wonderful young lady she was. It brought up emotion in me that I did not think existed.*

I also read your enclosed article from Guideposts magazine. That article gave me enough courage to write this letter even though I still cannot find a way to thank you in any way that really expresses all my feelings.

Prior to receiving Makenzie's heart, I was on the transplant list for a long time. Most of that time I felt mixed emotions about being on the list because I thought why should I benefit from someone else's tragic loss. I talked with my Chaplin about it. Her response was that "Nobody understands why things happen the way they do but you cannot feel guilty in the way He works. The family that makes the donation will want it to be a positive act and are donating it out of the kindness in their hearts."

I will never meet you or your family because of the transplant guidelines, but you all have my unending gratitude for your donation of Makenzie's heart. My prayers were with you and your family on June 4ᵗʰ even though I could not be at Makenzie's commemoration in celebration of her beautiful life.

I received Makenzie's heart on February 1ˢᵗ. It beats strong in my body. It saved my life. So far there have been no signs of rejection and I am feeling so much better than I have in a long time. It is a strong heart. I feel it beat and thank God every day for receiving it. I will take care of Makenzie's heart for the rest of my life like the treasure that it is. When I pray for the members of my family, I include Makenzie in those prayers. She is my life.

Thank you again and God bless you for your generosity in your time of suffering.

Larry

The bond that I share with Larry is so sweet. After all, he shares a piece of my heart. Through his letters he shares such a zest for life and he is actually very funny. He, like my husband Bob, loves to fish and like me, he enjoys writing. He certainly has a gift for writing and he is very entertaining in the way he writes. I recall when I first learned that a 70 year old man had received the gift of my daughter's heart. I was just so taken aback! How could this be that such a strong young heart would not be gifted to someone much younger? Remember, Makenzie was a very strong young soccer player. Physically fit. But, ah, I now understand and am so thankful that I "get it". God does not make mistakes! We feel honored that Larry is the caretaker of our daughter's heart. And such good care he is taking of it. Larry is so funny and apologetic when he writes his overdue letters and goes on to blame Makenzie for the delay because he had been busy fishing, or working around the yard, or repairing his roof.

I was glad when after three years of correspondence I finally convinced him that we needed to meet. Thank you, God and Larry, for this occasion. I chose the Magic Wings Butterfly Conservatory as a meeting spot for several reasons. First and foremost because my heart told me that was the perfect meeting place. Magic Wings is where Makenzie prepared her sixth grade science project years earlier. She interviewed the butterfly curator, asking questions about butterflies for her report and her Aunt Sherry came with us and took some beautiful photographs. Years later, at the graduation, mere months after we lost her, we purchased 77 monarchs from Magic Wings for a butterfly launch. Her friends came off the stage and let the monarchs go in her memory. It was lovely and inspirational. I felt it would be meaningful for the kids to have this positive reminder years later. Still to this date, her friends will send me a picture or a message letting me know they saw a butterfly and immediately thought of her.

Larry and I stay in touch via emails and he is such a pleasure to know. After meeting with Larry, I decided to ask him if he would be willing to share his story in a chapter for this book. He is such an eloquent and engaging writer and I thought it would be nice for others to get a sense of his journey through his illness and

Graduation Butterfly Launch

now his second chance at life with Makenzie's gift. He has titled this **Three Women**. Here is Larry's Story:

On February 1st 2010 I received a new heart that saved my life. I am sure that I am only alive today to write this story because of three women in my life.

One was a beautiful seventeen year old woman, named Makenzie, whose precious heart is now beating in my chest. Another woman is Marcy, Makenzie's mother, who made an agonizing, lonely, bittersweet decision to donate her daughter's organs to save other human lives. The third woman is my wife Mary who has saved me several times on our journey through life to get to this point.

Marcy asked if I would put some thoughts down to describe my experiences in receiving Makenzie's heart, so I thought I would introduce myself and describe how these three women got me here.

Before it all started

Glad to meet you—11.11.2013

My name is Larry. I am the grateful recipient of a heart transplant.

Like I said above, I was asked to write about how this life changing event has affected me. But before I do that I'd like to tell you a little bit about myself and the members of my family who were also affected. The people I care about most, my wife Mary and my three adult children; Kathy, Brian and Michael.

I met my wife one afternoon in 1956 at an ice skating rink when I was seventeen and she was thirteen. At that time I was working at the ice skating rink as a public skating monitor. My job was to keep the big kids from racing around the rink and to pick up littler skaters that had fallen and might get hurt by other skaters.

Just when things were going good and I thought the afternoon was going to be quiet, a young girl went racing by me and fell down right in front of me. I leaned down to help her up and got my hand slapped; she got up, brushed herself off, looked up at me and said "You knocked me down!" Her braces were the first thing that caught my eye.

I looked at her puzzled "I what?"

She put her hands on her hips and repeated "You knocked me down!"

I protested "I did not!"

And then my street mouth sprang into action "Nice braces, they're lighting up the rink!"

And she skated off leaving me confused. I thought, "why am I defending myself, I didn't do anything".

But I really knew why, even if I didn't realize it at the time. When I looked into her big blue eyes I knew right then and there I had met my soul mate. I saw her several more times at the rink that year, but four years difference in age, at that age, was a lot. We became friends and I saw her at a few school dances; you might say back then we were childhood sweethearts.

In those years everybody was expected to serve their country, so a year later I joined the Marine Corp. The next four years were dedicated to God, Country and Corp. We corresponded a few times by mail but I'm not much of a writer. I did stop at her house one rainy night while I was on leave to show off my uniform with its brand new PFC stripe sewn on.

She said "Your wool Marine coat smells in the rain."

Why does she always make me feel like I needed to defend myself? This time, since the Marine Corp had done everything in their power to make me a gentleman, I suppressed my street mouth.

Mary went to college while I was in the Corp and became a teacher. When I got out of the Corp I got a job and went to college at night and received a degree in electrical engineering. Magna Cum Laude I must say. I actually became a rocket scientist and worked on the electrical power plant for the Apollo moon space craft; but that's another story.

Guess what? Against all conceivable odds, blue eyes and I got married.

I never felt like this before

Heart Attack—11.20.1987

The tires slid on the wet fall leaves as the speeding car hurtled down the dark New England country road. The car fish-tailed once then bolted forward. I could see all this happening as I leaned back in the seat holding my chest. It was one of the few times in my life when I was definitely NOT in control.

My wife Mary was in the driver's seat leaning forward clutching the steering wheel, barking orders like my old First Sergeant, and pushing the gas pedal steady to the metal. We were on the way to the emergency room.

That afternoon was the end of a bright, beautiful fall day, and my family and I were outside raking oak leaves. They were dropping from the forty plus red oaks and pin oaks in our yard faster than we could remove them. Mary and I had rakes in our hands. Kathy our twenty-one year-old daughter who was studying to be a teacher at Westfield State College was home to help, and was lying on her back in a pile of leaves deciding which cumulus cloud looked more like the Pillsbury Dough Boy. My twelve-year-old son Mike, the intellectual, was leaning on a tree reading from his copy of **Tolkien's, The Lord of the Rings**. My sixteen-year-old middle son Brian, my right hand man, was in a steady and uphill battle to gain his sibling's attention long enough to pull the tarp full of leaves to the mulch pile.

At the end of the day, in the last light of the setting sun, our mulch pile cast a shadow that looked like the one cast by the great pyramid of Geisha, and the yard looked like it had never been raked. We were all beat and were sitting in our den rehashing the day and eating a well-deserved dish of ice cream when it happened.

I started to get a feeling of indigestion that stayed for a short time and went away. A few minutes later it came back but felt worse; but again it went away. After a while the pain came back and stayed. I never felt like this before. I had never been really sick before in my life and didn't want the kids to be alarmed, so I caught Mary's eye and left the room. She said "Get in the car Marine were going to the hospital".

So there I was holding my chest and Mary was swinging onto the main highway headed for the small local hospital. I had never been in a hospital before as a patient. Guess what? The pain went away. I told Mary, she said "We're still going to the hospital". It really did feel better.

At the hospital emergency room I was quizzed, poked, listened to and wired up to an EKG machine. I was right all along, nothing was wrong. EKG came back and showed no problem. The doctor said it was probably indigestion and that I could go home. I smiled. Mary put her hands on her hips and turned on the doctor. I'm beckoning to her in the background, let's go!

It seemed like a much longer ride home than when we went to the hospital. I was told so many times that I should have stayed in the hospital that I was thoroughly convinced by the time we pulled into our driveway that a night in the hospital wouldn't have been that bad.

The next night the same feeling came back. We headed to the hospital, but half-way there it went away, and I didn't want to be checked out again and sent home again, so I had Mary turn around. I don't know if she was driving really slowly, but it seemed like it took forever to reach our house.

The next day it started again. This time it was really bad. Mary called our family doctor. He said to call the hospital. They said "Get him to the hospital now"!!! When we got to the hospital I was in so much pain I could barely get out of the car. There was a nurse there with a needle full of morphine. She said "You'll feel a little pinch sir".

WOW! Holy Mother of God, did I feel good! I asked the nurse, "What is that stuff? I feel great; I think I can go home now".

The nurse replied "Just lie back, you're going to be here for a while". And I was. It was a massive heart attack. I spent a good while in the intensive care ward where I was assigned a great heart doctor. In time, I was transferred to telemetry and then to a regular floor, and eventually released with a whole new lifestyle assigned to me. I had to take lots of medicine and change my dietary habits. No more ice cream. No more smoking and lots of veggies. Nuts!

A big decision

Quadruple Bypass—05.14.1989

If there is one thing an old Marine can do, it's to practice self-discipline, given there is no other option. So I quit smoking and replaced ice cream with low fat yogurt. I started to read books on heart healthy diets and the types of aerobic exercises that would benefit my heart. The internet existed at that time but the World Wide Web would not be available to the public until around 1991 so I spent a lot of time reading books. They were just finding the relationships between cholesterol and saturated fats and how high amounts of sodium affected your heart. I learned how to cook low fat and low sodium meals. My cuisine was, as pointed out by my youngest son, Mike, "Blah, not very good is it". Not good tasting but edible. I also started an exercise program only matched, in my mind, by the legendary Rocky Balboa. I felt good. I think I kicked this problem.

Oh, oh, what's that feeling in my chest? It can't be. It was. A visit to the heart doctor verified that I had another heart related problem. I was scheduled for angioplasty. Yup, four arteries almost totally blocked. After eating all that blah food it was almost laughable. The doctor gave me some more information about the problem, which also didn't sound so good, and left me with a decision to make. I can still hear the heart doctor, "You can be back here next month with the same problems, only they will be worse, or you can have a bypass surgery".

A brief description of bypass surgery by the doctor, although presented delicately I'm sure, still sounded like "Well, they're going to rip your chest cavity open, tear some veins out of your legs, and replace a lot of parts, and then staple you together again. You have to decide if you want to do this right now".

It sounded good to me. "Um, OK, when can you do this for me"?

It sounded good to the doctors too. "Tomorrow morning."

And I got the last word, "Great"!!!

And that's how I decided to have my first by-pass surgery.

I love Gadgets

ICD Surgery—10.28.2002

The by-pass worked for me. I felt so much better and went back to work and life as normal. I did keep up the exercise and the restricted diet. You would be surprised what starts to taste good. Everything was going good until I had my regularly scheduled visit to our family doctor.

During my exam the doctor listened to my heart as usual. Then he listened again. Then said "You're heart is in atrial fibrillation. Go see your heart doctor, your heart isn't beating correctly, otherwise you're in good shape".

I thanked him, "It's nice to see you again too Doc."

So I saw my heart doctor. Guess what, I was in atrial fibrillation. He remarked, "You're heart is fibrillating; we can treat this to some extent with blood thinners but we should also look into a defibrillator."

Curious, I asked "What is a defibrillator"?

An all knowing response, "A defibrillator is a small electronic device embedded in your chest with wires that go through your veins into your heart. When you heart goes into fibrillation, an electronic pulse will shock your heart. I'm setting up an appointment with a specialist."

Great, I love gadgets.

So I saw the doctor that installed the defibrillators. He showed me a sample he had in his desk. It looked about the size of my flip-top cell phone with a socket on the end to stick wire leads into. This was a real gadget.

I asked, "And where are you going to put this"?

The doctor was beaming. "Well we're going to make a small incision right here in your upper chest near you left shoulder, place this device in the incision, and run leads down to your heart. Then we will close you up and set the proper parameters wirelessly".

Caught up in the euphoria of the moment I could only respond, "Let's do it"!

I do love gadgets.

What the Hell was that!

ICD Discharged—10.28.2003

I was standing in the river in my waders flipping a size 16 Blue-Winged-Olive dry fly at a rising trout about thirty feet away. It was a beautiful autumn afternoon and the fall colors were reflecting everywhere off the water. In my mind's eye, every cast I was making was perfect, the line made no splash, the nine foot leader material was invisible, and the fly looked perfect as it passed over the spot where the fish was rising. What was wrong with this fish? After about fifteen perfect presentations with no response, I hypothesized the fish was just plain ignorant and it could starve to death for all I cared. I decided I had enough fun for the day and stepped out of the stream.

There was a steep embankment to climb to get back to the road where my Ford Focus station wagon was parked, and I was a little bit out of breath as I opened the rear hatch back. I was holding my fishing rod in my left hand and the car keys in the other ....

ZZZZZZZZZaaaaaapppppppp!!!!!!!!!!!!!!!!!!!!!!!!!!!!!!!!!!! Flash of light!! Bolt of thunder!!

I guess I doubled over because when I woke up, the upper part of me was looking at the knees of my waders, and my fishing rod was sticking straight up in the air. I couldn't begin to understand what happened. In my fog, I looked up and saw some power lines overhead—my fishing rod must have hit the wires—although they are pretty high.

I sat down on the ledge of the hatch back and called my wife Mary to tell her what happened.

After she heard the story she said, "Your defibrillator fired; how are you feeling"?

I laughed, "There is no way that little device did this".

She said, "Get to the hospital".

I replied, "I'm not going to the hospital, I smell like fish".

Her reply, "You didn't catch any fish, go to the hospital. I'll meet you there".

The hospital checked out the device codes on the defibrillator. Guess what? It was that little device. I was sent home with the admonition to take it easy for a few days. I did, but every waking moment for the next few weeks held the expectation that my little zapper would find some other reason to give me another wakeup call.

Don't you just love gadgets?

Not again!

Heart Attack—01.06.2005

In January of 2005, Mary was again driving me to the hospital. No matter how well I took care of my body, my heart wasn't paying any attention. Like the Grinch, my heart had grown to three times its size. But unlike the Grinch, there was no room in my body for it. Because of all the damage done to my heart over the years, it had grown to compensate for that damage and had overgrown its capacity in my body.

There wasn't much they could do at the hospital except make me comfortable and let me rest. I was discharged later in the week.

Don't you just love a siren?

Heart Attack—03.07.2005

On March 7th of 2005 we were having a good ole New England late winter storm. It was about seven o'clock in the evening and there was about ten inches of heavy wet snow in the driveway. The plows had already passed by two times and left a three foot high impermeable barrier of snow, ice and slush at the end of our driveway.

Then I felt it one more time. There was a cramping pain in the chest and pain radiating down my arm. Mary saw my dilemma and how impossible it would be to get to the hospital. She dialed 911 and got the local police in town. In less than five minutes, they came crashing through the barrier at the end of the driveway and slid up the driveway to my house. They brought oxygen and other medical equipment and some much needed comfort. After assessing me, they radioed for the local ambulance.

The ambulance slid into the driveway and into the tracks left by the cruisers. Paramedics, with more equipment and a stretcher, slid me into the back of their ambulance. Off we went, sliding toward the local hospital. Then we slid off the main road and got stuck in the snow.

After a lot of radio traffic, I was told another ambulance from the hospital was on its way. I was transferred over the snow bank into the second ambulance and, in moments, we were back on our way. What I enjoyed most about this little adventure was the siren in the ambulance.

Don't you just love a siren?

You're going to do what?

Quadruple Bypass II—03.14.1989

After a week in the hospital, my cardiologist and the heart surgeon were sitting at the foot of my bed discussing the pros and cons of my future. Uh, hey guys I'm right here. My heart doctor was telling the surgeon, "He can't keep having heart attacks like this".

And the heart surgeon was saying, "In my assessment, he only has a fifty-fifty chance of surviving the operation".

My heart doctor countered with, "Doesn't everyone have that same chance in an operation"?

Good comeback Doc! Now that's why I like my cardiologist. I really didn't want another bypass, but I wanted my cardiologist to win, because he is such a nice guy.

The surgeon shrugged and said rather matter-of-factly "I'll schedule him as soon as possible".

We won!—I think.

Then I thought, "You're going to do what? Another bypass? I thought this was just a debate".

I had the bypass but things didn't go well this time. I had been taking a drug called Amioderone to regulate my heart fibrillations. And some people taking this drug before a bypass have lung problems after the bypass. Guess who was one of them?

My lungs collapsed and I had to be placed on high pressure oxygen. This caused a whole series of new problems that I won't go into here. Suffice it to say, I was in the hospital for months. And I was failing.

Finally Mary, hands on hips, told the doctors "I can take care of him better than you're doing at home".

Guess what? They discharged me in her care. I'm not sure if that was good or bad, but I got a lot of, "Get up and walk Marine! You're not going to just lay there". It took months of this before I got better.

You know, it's not getting any easier to bounce back from these operations the older I get. But be careful who you tell that to, especially if she has blue eyes.

A letter from my doctor

Heart Donor List—Year 2008

"How's the fishing", my cardiologist asked during my regular checkup.

"I keep them frightened" I smiled.

In the year 2008 I had my semi-annual checkup with my cardiologist. I think we both liked these checkups because my cardiologist liked gadgets too. He had purchased a rack of electronic instruments that could assess and change parameters on defibrillators. After the normal checkup, he would hang this WiFi receiver over my shoulder and across my defibrillator so that the instruments could read from it.

My doctor exclaimed, "Oh, look there, your heart is in fibrillation right now. Let's amplify that and get a better look. How about that? Look at how it can show you the shape of the heart pulse in real time"!

I chimed in, "Let's freeze it and print out a hard copy".

We both enjoyed that part; pawing over the printouts.

After we fooled around some more with the electronics, my doctor removed the WiFi reader and sat back. "I wrote a letter to the transplant clinic to see if you can be assed for a heart transplant. This heart is not going to last much longer".

I replied, "Um, don't you think I'm getting a little old for this"?

"You're in good shape. I'm going to send the letter", he said as he slid his chair behind his desk.

So the transplant clinic got a letter from my doctor.

What's this stuff?

Start Milrinone—01.08.2008

I went to Boston for my evaluation. I stayed there about a week and was poked, prodded, and drained of most of my blood, needle by needle. They evaluated me for all diseases known to mankind both physical and mental.

Finally the evaluation team came back with the answer. I would be put on the transplant list, with some sort of status that I never really understood, even though I nodded my head a lot as if I did. Note: if you want to look intelligent, keep your mouth shut and casually nod you head. It works for me.

So when they said, "We are going to start you on Milrinone to keep your heart healthy while you wait for a transplant". I simply nodded and smiled.

That was when, what they call a PIC nurse came into my room with a cart full of dangerous looking instruments and a mask over her face. It was time to start asking questions. I asked, "What's that stuff"?

The muffled answer was, "I'm going to run this tube into your arm and up your blood vessel into your heart".

Now was the time to show ignorance. "How are you going to do that"?

"Well, first I'm going to measure the length of your arm, so I'll know how much tube we will need, then I will insert the catheter into your vein with a needle", she explained, as my arm was being washed and disinfected prior to launch.

Then as I was mulling this all over, she did it. Wow, she was quick with that tube. The next thing I knew, they were dripping the Milrinone solution into my heart. Then the PIC nurse packed up her gear and rolled it out of the room. She never unmasked, and I wonder if anybody knows who the PIC nurse is.

After a few days of monitoring, they let me go home with the strictest warnings about getting an infection and how it could get into my body easily through the PIC line opening. At home I had a visiting nurse change the PIC line dressing every day to keep it clean. But I'm an outdoor kind of guy and before lone the dreaded infection got me. Back to the hospital to see the masked nurse, get a new PIC line, kill the infection. Stern warnings were issued by all.

This happened three times before the "team" decided PIC lines weren't for me. A Hickman device was the answer. This is a catheter inserted through your chest wall and into your heart. No exposure to the elements and with two ports. It had an "In" and an "Out" port. It was neat, they could pump Milrinone in the In-port and take blood samples from the Out-port. And it did work great, believe it or not, no more infections.

However, looking at my chest with scars from neck to belly button, an implanted defibrillator below my left shoulder and a Hickman device below my right shoulder wasn't a pretty site. My Dermatologist remarked after I took off my tee shirt, "All you need now are electrical bolts in your neck".

Here for the duration

Admitted to Hospital—10.15.2009

On October 15, 2009 I was admitted to the hospital. Mary and I drove to Boston that morning for my regular checkup where they took blood samples, assessed my heart, and of course checked the Hickman device. As I pushed the button for the elevator I suddenly felt real lighted headed. Mary asked if I was OK and grabbed my elbow.

I said, "Yeah, a little dizzy. It's probably the fasting for the blood work and the long drive to get here. This will go away after we stop for lunch".

My life long partner quipped, "You've always been a little dizzy", as we got on the elevator.

By the time we got to the doctor's office, I felt much better and had the usual doctor patient dialog. These were all great doctors at the transplant clinic and they explained in minute detail what was happening to you without pulling any punches. I liked that.

The doctor listened to my heart. Then he listened again. Then he went to my back and listened again. Then he had me lay back and listened again. Then he stepped back and said, "You're not leaving this hospital today. You're not leaving until we get you a new heart".

I didn't know what that meant or what it would entail; all I could think of at the moment was how Mary was going to get home alone through all the Boston traffic.

The doctor explained that I would be given a room in the Cardiomyopathy ward and that someone would come and take me there. I sat in the doctor's office waiting for what will happen next. Mary knew this was not making me happy; she tried to encourage me, "Maybe this is the best thing that could happen".

"Fishing would be the best thing that could happen". I snapped.

Then a young man showed up with a wheelchair that changed my day. God always seems to send someone to help you out, a Haitian. I always loved the Haitian Creole accent. "Hop in mon, I get you where you're going". He made me feel comfortable. He knew every doctor, nurse and hospital worker we passed. We talked; he assured me that I was in good hands at this hospital. In my book, that was better than any hospital rating system. When he dropped me off at my destination we shook hands and he said he would check on me later.

And he did. Later that night after I was checked in and lying in bed he poked his head in my room, "Howse my mon toonaite"? He had a lemon frozen-ice for me. I got to know him well over the next three and a half months, along with the food staff and the room cleaning crew. They are all great people, and quite helpful, since they run the hospital underground. You need extra stuff, they can get it.

The next morning Grey's Anatomy showed up en masse. They stood, sat, and leaned on the walls, as the head doctor (a great guy BTW), discussed the condition of my heart. In a nutshell, my heart was bad and I needed to be stabilized and monitored while I was there. He explained, "We need to know how your heart is functioning. To do that, we need to measure the pressure in your heart along with a lot of other parameters. This team will take care of all that".

I ventured, "And how is it done"?

One of the wall-leaning doctors explained, "Well we need to place a pressure measuring device in your heart. This is done by making a small opening in your carotid artery and inserting a line that will be located in your heart using an imaging scope".

Sweet!

"Then we will connect wires to the probe and they will be hooked up to the monitoring devices over your bed. You'll be able to move from the bed to the chair in your room if you're careful with the wires".

Double sweet! Just wonderful!

Within the hour, I was in the imaging room with a doctor holding a scalpel, and three imaging technicians. An hour later I was back in my room hooked up to my monitoring machines. Every week the procedure was repeated to put a new probe in my neck. You know, I was starting to lose my interest in new gadgets.

I won't belabor you with how I whiled away my time in this condition; I will just say it gives you a lot of time to think about life and how precious it is. I'm sure my case is not unique; in fact, the patient in the next room over was like this for almost a year. The hospital staff knows this condition is not pleasant and offers a lot of support. We had special meals on Thanksgiving and Christmas and Santa's elves left gifts beside our beds while we slept on Christmas night (I have my suspicions it was the night nurse).

The hospital Chaplain and I became good friends. She would visit once or twice a week and we would have long talks about life, death and heart transplants. I could not get over the fact that someone would have to die so that I could live. It just didn't seem ... right, I guess.

In one of our conversations she told me, "It is not your decision who the Lord takes and who he spares. If you don't receive the donated heart, someone else on the list will receive it. Your only decision at this point is will you put yourself in the hands of the Lord"?

She went on "Nobody understands why things happen the way they do but you cannot feel guilty in the way He works. The family that makes the donation will want it to be a positive act and are donating it out of the kindness in their hearts".

So I put myself in the hands of the Lord. And I waited.

Saved.

Heart transplant—01.02.2010

The morning of February 1st started off differently. After you have been in the hospital for a while, you get sort of a sixth sense about the environment. This morning the nurses were overly attentive, there was no "Come on, get out of that bed and enjoy the world. Not every place has this kind of stimulating view from their window". They were quiet, too quiet. They weren't telling me something. I wasn't getting any eye-to-eye contact. It was like they wanted me to know something but couldn't say.

It wasn't long before the **Grey's Anatomy** arrived. Everybody was smiling, "We think we have a donor. We are still doing some matching, but we're pretty sure. Don't have any breakfast this morning".

Two hours later, I was on a gurney headed for the operating room. They put me to sleep. The last thing I remember; countless doctors and staff, all masked, moving quickly around the room.

I woke up in intensive care. The Hickman device with the "In" and "Out" ports was gone. The defibrillator was gone. And I could hear a new heart beating in my chest.

I was saved!

I didn't know it at the time, but a second woman had just entered my life to save it—Makenzie.

Complications

Two days later I was back on the main floor. I felt great. I was ready to get out of there and get home. Then I started to feel starved of breath. It got worse quickly. The nurses saw my condition and called the team in to take a look. They called a Code Blue. In less than five minutes, I was sedated, on oxygen and being wheeled back to the operating room. I was not conscious when I arrived. They had to open my chest up again.

Again I woke up in the intensive care wing with a tube sticking straight up out of my mouth. It is called endotracheal intubation. You cannot make this stuff up. I found a distinct dislike for this tube over the next five days. Intubation, in the simplest terms is a long, wide tube taped to a stick and stuffed down your throat. You lay on your back, you can't move. And they put a large ticking clock on the wall right in front of you. Someone checks on you several times a day. That's you're entertainment.

Tick, tick, tick. Five days. Five nights. Nobody really tells you what's going on. You can only sleep so much. You have a lot of time to think.

I can hear my new heart. It's strong and really beating great. It gives me hope just listening to it. I didn't know at that time whose heart it was but I knew this heart was strong. I'm not giving up. No way.

This stick is driving me nuts. I'm going to smash that clock when they untie me from this bed!

They finally took the tube out of my throat. I spent two more days in ICU while they verified that my breathing was OK. The test was; could I lift a ball to a certain height by blowing in a tube. I pegged the ball up against the stops. I wanted out.

I was returned to the main floor and a week later I was released from the hospital in Mary's care. I was never so glad to see those blue eyes.

I never knew what the complication was.

Recovery

Home—February 2010

At my age, recovering from three and a half months of inactivity was not easy. Makenzie's heart was doing great, but getting back the strength in the rest of my muscles came slowly. Mary, my drill sergeant, was always there to make sure my daily exercise routines were carried out in full. And in time, I could do as much as I wanted without getting tired and overwhelmed by the effort.

There were ten weekly visits to Boston for biopsies to verify that there was no rejection. Yup, through the carotid artery again, but I was so familiar with doctors and nurses in the imaging lab it was like ole home week for me. Fortunately, the biopsies all showed zero rejection characteristics. Even the doctors were somewhat surprised at what a perfect match Makenzie's heart was to my body. I wound up requiring very little rejection medicine. Someone was watching over me.

All this time I was being reminded by the doctors and nurses that a letter of thanks to my donor's family would be nice. I kept telling them I would send one, but it wasn't true. I didn't know what to say to the family who lost a loved one, especially since I knew I could never express my gratitude in any manner that reflected my true feelings. I was stuck for words.

Marcy

Letters—May 2010

On May 18th 2010, Marcy wrote to me. (I later learned that this was Makenzie's birthday). It was forwarded to me through the donor association's letter exchange program. It was a short letter introducing herself and telling me about her family and Makenzie, the beautiful young woman whose heart was donated to save another person in need. Along with the letter was enclosed an article titled "A Gift of Hope" from **Guideposts**. The article was about an organ donor's mother and the woman who received the donated organ. It described the thoughts and emotions of both women and the difficulty they had in writing their first letters to each other.

I was amazed to find that I had almost the exact same feelings as the organ recipient in the article; she couldn't find the right words to say either. However, the next day after reading Marcy's letter and the **Guidepost** article, I sprang into action; brought up Microsoft Word on my computer, and in only one month responded to Marcy's letter. As I look back, it was a lame letter, but again in my defense, it only took one month to compose.

We started to correspond with each other on a more regular basis and I could feel the pain Marcy was feeling coming right off the pages of her letters. She never described her pain, but I could feel it. She told me about Makenzie's friends and how comforting they were to her, about how

Makenzie's school made her a memorial, about Makenzie's boyfriend and about Makenzie's life. Marcy was in pain. I assumed from her writings that Marcy was about the age of my daughter and I just felt like holding her and letting her cry it out. But I didn't say that in the letters I wrote back. I wrote back with more of my superbly crafted prose about fly-fishing and other equally stimulating nothingness. What is wrong with me?

Magic Wings—October, 2013

In one of her letters Marcy asked if we could meet. In the donor program, both the donor family and the organ recipient must both agree that a meeting should take place. It all seemed a little restricting to me but I'm sure there are reasons for the donor association's caution. Anyway, I agreed, and Marcy and I exchanged email addresses to make corresponding easier. So after several emails, we decided to meet at a place called Magic Wings, which was one of Makenzie's favorite places. I told Mary about the plans to meet Marcy; she looked at me and said, "That's nice, and for God's sake get a haircut before you meet anybody".

The foliage season in our area of New England in the autumn of 2013 was the longest and most colorful I had seen in many years. We had just enough sun, rain, warm days, freezing nights, and frost to coax every last bit of color from the trees. It started in late September and ended about the first week of November and Mary and I had spent quite a few days driving to different locations to enjoy the color. The hillsides looked like a Disney movie with little individual puff balls of various colors covering the landscape.

It was a good time to think about what I would say to Marcy when we met, how I could thank her. I find one of the best places for me to think is where I fly fish, so I asked Mary if she would like to take a trip there to see the color. We brought the Sunday paper with us so Mary could read while I walked the banks of the stream. Mary is not big on bugs, snakes, or bear sightings, so she settled in the car overlooking the river and read the paper. I walked the banks of the stream to a point where the stream widened and the water slowed down before it flowed over a natural rock dam. I sat on a log and watched the various colored leaves pass by on the surface of the water. They still had small beads of water on them from the frost we had the night before, and the sun reflected off them like small bright lights. The slowly floating leaves with the reflecting beads of light looked like an armada of brightly colored ships heading off to do battle, as in Homer's Odyssey. Each ship contained its own warriors with glints of light reflecting off their swords and spears as they headed toward the rock dam where the Sirens were calling and where they would do battle.

This is ridiculous, Homer? I could think of nothing appropriate that I could say to Marcy to tell her how I felt. Then as I got up to leave, it dawned on me that maybe I should offer Marcy a chance to feel Makenzie's heart beating in my chest. I didn't want to offend Marcy in any way but it was all that I could think to offer. When I got back to the car, I asked Mary what she thought because she always knew more about these things than I did. Mary leaned over to put the paper on the car floor in front of her and stayed there for moment thinking. She straightened up, looked at me, and with a little choke in her voice said, "That is what I would have wanted".

On the way home Mary said, "Get a haircut". I didn't. As much as I love gadgets, I hate haircuts.

I had never been to Magic Wings, but Marcy said there was a waiting area in the building and we could meet there. So when I arrived I parked my car in the parking lot and went inside into the lobby waiting area. I had never met Marcy before and didn't know who I was looking for, but there was a woman sitting on a bench in the lobby that looked like she was waiting for someone. I approached her and said "Hi, Marcy"? The woman clutched her pocket book closer to her body and said "No". The look about her said I probably should have gotten a haircut. I decided to wait outside for Marcy. After I had walked the length of the building, I turned around and saw a young woman about to enter the building. She stopped when she saw me and said, "Larry"? I probably looked a little overeager at this point as I said, "Yes". I started to think; I really, really should have gotten a haircut. But, after I talked to Marcy a few minutes I found that I was really at ease with this woman.

Magic Wings is an awesome place. Once you enter into the semi-tropical world, you find yourself immersed in a surrounding of unusual and wondrous sights. There are butterflies, and I mean there are a lot of butterflies, and giant moths, and thirty-foot-tall pieces of grass that look like mature trees. There are small white quail running across your path, and tropical growth growing over your head on any path you take; boxes of pupating and hatching butterflies and iguanas in cages, and ornate park benches along the way where you can sit and take in all that is around you, and fish in pools beneath your feet. It was my kind of place. I'm going to have to go back someday.

After Marcy gave me a tour of the place, we sat on one of the park benches in an alcove under a tropical tree, and Marcy asked if I had the time to look at some things she had brought along. I said yes, and she asked me to wait there while she got them. When she returned, she had a shopping bag with a picture album and a scrapbook album. She opened the Picture album and I placed it across my lap so I had a good view of the pictures.

They were pictures of Makenzie's life. There were pictures of Makenzie and her girlfriends at all kinds of events and in each picture you could see just how much Makenzie was enjoying life with her friends. In almost every picture Makenzie would stick her tongue out at the camera or make a funny face while she and her friends were playing at different things. This was a girl that enjoyed life; enjoyed people, enjoyed doing silly and crazy things. Page after page I turned to a new adventure in her short life. She was a beautiful child and a beautiful young woman, and I could feel nothing but a sense of loss in this world for not having her anymore. I said nothing or very little as I turned the pages. When the last page turned, Marcy folded the books and we talked for a while until it was time to leave.

I offered to carry the albums for her as we left Magic Wings and headed for our cars. When we reached Marcy's car, we exchanged short goodbye pleasantries and I took a step back. I looked at Marcy and decided to offer the only gift I had left to offer. I didn't know how Marcy would react but I said "Marcy, would you like to feel Makenzie's heart beat"?

Relief swept through me when she said, "I'm glad you asked; I was just about to ask you if I could". I choked down a tear as Marcy put her hand on my chest. Then Marcy looked up at me and asked if she could listen to Makenzie's heart. I nodded yes because at that point I was so choked up I couldn't speak. I was not going to let this brave woman see a grown Marine weep. Marcy listened for a time then stepped back and said, "Thank you so much Larry". And she turned and headed for her car. I watched as Marcy's car left the lot and thought for a long time before I started my car and left. I prayed that Marcy thought me a worthy recipient of her daughter's heart.

I Hear You Knocking

"Snowtober"—October 2011

On October 29, 2011, a Halloween nor'easter, now referred to as "Snowtober", bore down on New England with hurricane force winds and record snowfalls. Most trees at that time were still in leaf and the extra weight of the snow and high winds caused trees to collapse, causing extensive power line damage. Major storm damage and power losses occurred in 12 states and three Canadian provinces. On October 31, 2011 New Englanders awoke to a bright sunshiny day with 10 to 30 inches of snow and a devastated infrastructure.

While Marcy and I were talking on that bench at Magic Wings I told her of an experience I had that may or may not have any bearing on our combined experience. First of all, let me say that I am not a believer in paranormal experiences, but I have had an event happen to me that makes me at least question my disbelief. Since I feel at risk of losing all my credibility, I will tell you that this is only being included at the request of Marcy, after we talked at Magic Wings.

It happened in October 2011, just weeks before the storm described above. I was lying in bed one night reading a story involving my favorite storybook character, a fictional FBI agent called Aloysius X. L. Pendergast, when I heard a knock coming from somewhere close by. I arose and donned my slippers to find the source of the knocking, which was persisting and getting more intense. It seemed to be coming from within the wall of the upstairs bathroom. I walked around trying to locate the source. The wall separated the bathroom from a closet in an adjacent bedroom. I searched the closet thoroughly, looking for any method that might cause such a knock. I found none. I put my ear to the bathroom wall to pin point the source. It was emanating from a location about a foot above the light switch. The first thing I thought of was, it was an animal in the wall, but it really did not sound like an animal. It sounded like someone knocking with a knuckle within the wall. The next thing I thought was that I was nuts; and just then the knocking stopped and I returned to bed.

Having been involved in research most of my life, the first thing I did was try to analyze the problem. First of all, I had watched over the construction of the house from the basement on up and I knew that this section of wall didn't contain any piping. I also knew that it was sealed at the top and bottom and on all sides by two-by-four studding. The only pass-troughs into the wall were wires and they generally don't knock. So like most good researchers who can't resolve a problem, I gave up and returned to Pendergast.

I told Mary about the knocking the next day. She remarked, "Right". She didn't believe me! Two nights later the knocking returned. This time I called "Miss Skeptic" away from the TV and asked her to come and listen. She did, she said, "It's a squirrel". It's not important what she said, what's important is that she heard the knocking too. I'm really not nuts.

I can tell you right now it wasn't a squirrel. I've had squirrels in the attic before. When you have squirrels you know it. They run along the rafters, they chatter, they invite friends in, they make a mess, and they drive you out of your mind. This wasn't squirrels.

In retrospect, I had a smart phone sitting on my desk with a recorder function; I could have recorded the knocking. Unfortunately I didn't, and now I don't know if there was a message in the knocking or not. The knocking got more frequent as the end of October approached.

Then the October storm hit. I live in a house surrounded by large oak trees, and Mary and I spent the whole night looking for a safe place in the house, as trees and tree branches came crashing down all around us. We could hear branches crashing on the roof and in the yard and scraping down the side of our house. The power in our town goes out all the time, and this night it had gone out many hours before the storm actually hit. It was cold in our house that night and Mary and I were bundled up in coats and huddled under blankets in our living room. The living room side of our house had the least amount of trees and it was our best option.

In the middle of all this, I heard the knocking begin again coming from the bathroom wall upstairs, but this time it was fierce. I mean I thought the knocking was going to break a hole in the wall. I went to the foot of the stairs but the knocking was so fierce that I didn't want to go up. Just then, one of the giant oaks in the back of the house broke away at the base and the whole tree came crashing through the roof. The bulk of the tree fell right on the wall where the knocking was coming from.

Mary and I spent the rest of the night huddled together praying for the best. The next morning I crept up the stairs to examine the damage. There was a two foot diameter tree trunk laying on the bathroom wall, and quite a large hole in the roof, with snow melting in the upstairs tub.

We had a new roof put on the house because there were so many holes punched through it from the tree branches falling on it. The contractor said the tree broke six to eight roof rafters and was really stopped by the bathroom wall.

Now you might say this is all just happenstance and you might be right. But just to add more kindling to the fire, about two weeks after the house was repaired and all was being forgotten, the knocking returned. This time it wasn't from the bathroom wall, it was from within my closet next to the bed. It wasn't loud and it didn't last long, just a few taps followed by a few more. Maybe it was a goodbye since I haven't heard anything since; or maybe I am a nut.

Or maybe, just maybe, it was a young lady keeping her heart safe.

Larry at Magic Wings Butterfly Museum

Chapter Three

A Great Escape-A Visit from Ten Besties

We have a summer seasonal camp in a campground in New Hampshire. It is close to the ocean and is situated in a very busy area, so lots to do. The camp had become a great escape for me in the beginning; an environment where I did not have to worry about bumping into friends and acquaintances which would place me in a position to convince people that everything was o.k. It wasn't for quite some time. I took long solo walks on the beach and in the woods and was able to think and cry and cry some more. We had only been in that campground for a few years so had not yet established many close friendships. I use to tell Bob, "It is you and me against the world". What I meant was that he was my closest confident, my rock, and my world. I felt like we were going through the motions but I really did not feel connected to my life as I knew it.

Over the years, we have developed a sincere appreciation for the place we call our second home. It is a very happy place, as it should be. People are on vacation taking much needed rest and enjoying family time. I feel glad that I raised my children camping. Although it was not in this campground, it was equally, if not more, our happy place. My son looks forward each summer to coming to the beach and loves to camp. I laugh when I think of Sean's love for campfires. He tends to get carried away and builds these very big campfires that will burn for hours on end. I also enjoy when he asks me if I have kite string and an onion bag because I know what he is planning, even now as an adult. When our children were very young someone had suggested that we take our kids crabbing. We would take onion bags, those red bags with more holes than the twine they are made up of. We placed some small rocks into the bags, added bologna and or hotdogs, and then tied the top of the onion bags with kite string. We took the kids down to the docks at the marina and watched them drop the onion bags into the water off the dock. Within seconds, crabs grabbed a hold of the bags in an attempt to get at the food inside. The kids loved fishing for crabs in this fashion. They would raise the bags up and drop them onto the dock and allow all the crabs to jump onto the dock and scurry back into the water. This entertained the kids for hours.

During that first summer after Kenzie left us, I made friends by painting rocks. There is a lovely rock beach that I frequent in Rye, NH. It overlooks the raw, rough, seacoast and the scenery is simply breathtaking. We go there because we can park our car along the coastline and walk to this rock filled beach. Beach lovers and sun bathers simply do not want to set up their blankets on rocks. Bob and I however, are willing to climb down huge boulders, carrying beach chairs, fishing gear, and of course a good book simply to have the isolated area to ourselves. Our own piece of heaven as we are surrounded by rocks and can enjoy the music of the waves crashing against them as the tide slips in. We find the most beautiful rocks there. They are smooth from the water and we have found so many interesting shapes. I always collect a few to take back to the camp with us. When there is nothing to do at the camp, I will set up my paints outside on the picnic table. I have invited people walking by our campsite to come paint a rock with me. It is a nice relaxing way to enjoy company and to get to know someone better. I also ask our guests who come to visit us if they will paint a rock. We have numerous painted rocks. I keep them all and can pretty much remember who painted each one. The rocks provide a memory of the time that each friend visited.

Makenzie's friends came up to the camp that first summer. Because she had ten besties, I asked them to come in two smaller groups to better accommodate them at the camp. The girls are wonderful and were so kind to me. I would think that they would have had better things to do at age 18 than to come paint rocks and string beads with Kenzie's mom, but they came. I feel so incredibly blessed to have had that time with each of them, getting to know them better. By spending time with her friends, it was almost like spending time with her. I believe that her friends took the same comfort by spending time with me. They told me that my daughter and I shared a few of the same mannerisms, and at times I think that they found it amusing.

A funny thing happened when I was shopping to prepare for the second group of friends to arrive. The first group had come and gone, and our time together was wonderful. I went shopping at a mega supermarket to buy food and snacks for the next group of friends. When I was in the freezer section of the store, I was shopping for ice cream. There was one other person in the aisle with me. All of a sudden something flew down from the ceiling and dropped at my feet. The gentleman at the other end of the aisle even commented that things were falling from the sky for me. I bent over and picked the box up. It was a box of blueberry pop tarts. This was significant to me as one of Kenzie's favorite snacks was pop tarts. She and Kayla would enjoy toasted pop tarts in her room when Kayla slept over.

Friends: (back): Alyssa, Casey, (front): Jordan, DJ, and me

Friends: (left to right): Nicole, Chelsey, Ashley, Francesca, Meghan

Chapter Four

God Winks, Nothing by Chance

...Yet I will not forget you. See, I have inscribed you on the palms of My hands... Isaiah 49:15b-16a.

In the beginning, there were so many little reminders that she left for me. Although I say it matter-of-factly that Makenzie left me these reminders, I must add that I believe that God provided these small gifts to help me stay positive. I thank my Father in heaven for His blessings and share them with you as a testament to my faith in Him.

Three days or so after she left us, I found one of the first signs. Years earlier, Kenz and I watched the movie Phantom of the Opera at my sister's house. We enjoyed it immensely. I bought the DVD and gave it to Makenzie in her Christmas stocking the following year but she never opened it. She told me that she wanted to wait and watch it with Kayla, her best friend. She stored this unopened DVD on the shelf under her television, in her room, with all the other DVDs. Anyhow, on this particular day very soon after she passed, I walked into her room and saw the DVD lying on the DVD player opened; out of its wrapper. This stopped me in my tracks.

One morning, just a week or so after Makenzie's funeral, I woke up and went into the kitchen to find an unusual sight. I had previously taken a few of the large roses from one of the funeral arrangements and bound them together and placed them in a vase of water in the center of the kitchen table. I found the roses upside down on the table with their stems in the air several inches from the vase. I asked my husband if he had taken them out of the vase and put them upside down on the table as a joke. He had not. Another time when I awoke, I came in to the kitchen to see her friend Nicole's picture upside down on my refrigerator door. We certainly did not place it there upside down. This made me laugh. I repositioned it right side up but this continued to happen for several days following.

Finding Dimes—"10" Lives on!

Makenzie told me that after her friend Danielle's grandmother died that Danielle kept finding dimes everywhere. Danielle and her grandmother had always saved dimes together. I suppose that is why I seem to find a spare dime when needed most. Maybe it's also because Makenzie's soccer number was 10. When I find myself thinking hard about her, a dime seems to mysteriously find its way into my path. One of those times was when I was meeting Felicia, Kenzie's kidney recipient. I was very nervous parking at the train station and very emotional. As I got out of the car and was closing my door, I noticed a dime on the seat where I had been sitting. Yes, dimes make me smile. One evening when Trevor, my little grandson was staying over, I was putting him to bed and he asked if he could sleep with the Santa Pig. Do you remember the Build a Bears stores at the shopping malls? As a young girl, Makenzie had gone shopping with a friend and purchased one of those, only it was a build a pig. She had purchased a Santa outfit for it and we referred to it as the Santa Pig. Anyhow, as I was saying good night to Trev, I tucked him in with the Santa Pig and kissed him goodnight. I left his room and collapsed on the living room couch and cried. Big sobs, big heaving sobs. As I sat there I felt as if something pushed up on the back of the couch against me. It felt almost like a person was there pushing me. I spun around but nothing was there. I moved the cushions and there it was-a dime!

Still years later, I continue to find dimes on my way to visit her bench to water flowers, and recently a trip to go Parasailing. I was a little nervous as I dressed in my "traveling Kenzie T-shirt" getting ready to fly high in the sky wearing it. As I returned to my cup of coffee, I found a dime sitting next to it. I even found a dime in the boot I was wearing as I was heading out of work one day. I had just commented the day before that I had not seen any signs from her recently; then this, even after five years.

Another Wink with a Whinny

We gave my grandson Trevor a little rocking horse for his first Christmas. When you push the button in the little pony's ear, it whinnies and makes galloping sounds. Very cute, but Trevor was just a baby and too young to activate it. I remember one afternoon when he was at our house napping, I heard sounds from his nursery. I went in and he was lying there in his crib laughing. In the corner of his room the little rocking horse was whinnying and galloping. This actually happened quite often. One time Bob was chasing the dogs around the couch in the living room and we heard the horse starting its antics in the baby's room. No one was in there. Another time, I was putting clean sheets in Trevor's crib and the little pony started. Another time, Matt, Makenzie's boyfriend had come for a visit and it started while we were sitting in there visiting. I decided it was time for the little pony to take a vacation. I sent it home with Trevor's mom to keep it for a couple of weeks. She returned it to me later saying that she heard nothing from it. She had placed the horse in the back of my SUV when I met her as I was returning Trevor after a sleep-over. That evening, Bob and I decided to go out for dinner. He drove his truck up to get a haircut and we had agreed that I would drive up to the hair salon in my vehicle and meet him, and we would go on to the restaurant from there. Bob came out of the hair salon and jumped into my car. I looked at him and said: "You look hot"! Wouldn't you know, the little rocking horse in the back of my SUV started whinnying and galloping. Bob and I looked at each other and laughed.

There was the time when I was riding with some new friends to my first regional meeting in my new business endeavor with **Nerium International**. My friend Julie W. was driving us there and she asked me to share with these new friends a little bit about Makenzie. As I explained that my daughter shared her organs and saved lives, I noticed a word scroll across Julie's radio. Julie has one of those Sirius radios that will display the name of the artist and the song that is playing. As I was speaking about my daughter, the word "Butterflies" scrolled across the radio screen. I just smiled to myself and thought hmmm, wonder if there is a song or a band named butterflies. Anyway, I said nothing of it to these new friends. After our meeting as we headed home, the conversation again ended up on Kenzie and I started sharing some of the funny little reminders that are given to me. As I was sharing, another word scrolled across Julie's radio screen in her car. This time the word was MARCY in all capital letters, (my name!). I gasped this time and they all asked what was wrong. I asked if any of them had seen my name scroll across the radio screen. As I said it, it appeared again and again, maybe five times or so and they all saw it. Imagine, what are the odds that a song title or artist named Marcy would scroll across the radio screen. Now, I tell people that I am living life with "Eyes and Heart Wide Open" as I continue to see these little or, not so little, reminders.

Another time as I was sweeping my floor, my eyes caught a tiny white something on the floor. I picked it up to look closer; it was the word angel. I love that. Of course I immediately took a picture of it on my phone and posted the pic on social media. I have been told by so many friends that they adore my posts when my daughter leaves her calling card. Norma, my friend commented on my post and I wanted to share it here. She wrote: **"God Winks; Nothing by Chance".** That was the first time that I had ever heard that expression, and it seemed so appropriate.

Even after five years, we continue to get the reminders. I received a phone call and a text from my friend Pam. Pam explained that she was very emotional the night before as she noticed an unopened box that had landed in her hallway as they were doing renovations in her home. She said that right on top of the box was a CD Mix that Makenzie had created. She played the CD and all of the songs were speaking to her. Here is the text that she sent to me:

Marcy!! Here is a picture of the CD...the Mix by Kenzie! The first song is from Rent. The song talks about measuring your life in love. I love you sweetheart! I feel like Kenzie is talking to us all through her song choices here.

One day I was in the lobby of the local hospital looking at sales items on a cart outside the gift shop. There was another woman there and we were laughing at one of the gadgets there on the cart when my phone just started playing a song very loudly. (For the life of me, I do not remember the song which I usually like to pay heed to, as its message is always perfect). I was so focused on shutting down the music and honestly had no idea why it was playing as I had not opened any music apps on my phone. I looked at the woman standing there with me, and giggled as the lobby of the hospital was very quiet, other than my blaring phone. I commented to her that it must be my daughter trying to get my attention. As I shut the phone off, I explained to her that I had lost my daughter in a tragic accident and that I find sometimes things are used to get my attention. The woman's eyes were as big as marbles as she gasped! I ased her what was wrong and she explained to me that her sister had just lost her teenage daughter a month earlier. We talked a bit about it and I asked how she was doing. I should know better, such a dumb question but, it is just what people ask to politely inquire. I knew firsthand how she was doing.

For me, probably the first few months I would say, there wasn't a day that went by that I did not think about jumping off a bridge to end my sadness. Of course I knew better. If I wanted assurance of ever seeing my girl again, this was not my answer. So I asked this woman who I had just met, if she would like me to reach out to her sister by writing a letter. And so I did, and eventually talked with her on the phone. This mother, who had just lost her daughter, happened to be the wife of a pastor. She was mad at God. I've been told this is not an uncommon emotion when the biggest gift ever given to you, your child, is taken away!

And so the letter writing continues. I continue to write letters to people who I do not know to let them know that I am praying for them and to invite them to make contact if they wish to speak or just hang out with someone who has and is walking in their same shoes. I have made many acquaintances and friends this way. Although it might not have been a ministry that I would have chosen for myself, I believe that God is using me for His purpose in this manner.

When Trevor was just an infant, maybe a month or so old, I was given the sweetest gift of taking care of my new born grandchild a few days a week. He even slept over a couple of nights each week as it made it easier on his mom on those early mornings when she needed to get to work. At times I got melancholy thinking about my children and how I missed out on their infancy due to having to go right back to work so soon after they were born. I recall one afternoon sitting in the rocking chair in the nursery giving Trevor a bottle before his nap and rocking him while I wept. I was so missing my girl. I sobbed for a bit and then looked up and saw this silly little picture that Makenzie had pasted to the wall. It was a picture of a donkey and she had superimposed her own picture to make it appear as if she were riding the donkey. I started to laugh. Our girl had a gift for making people laugh. As Trevor had fallen asleep, I placed him in his crib and walked over to the mirror on the wall to check my makeup since I was sure that I was quite the sight after crying some big tears. To my amazement, there was a little fortune pasted to the mirror. Makenzie liked to save her fortunes from the Chinese fortune cookies and I continue to find them here and there when least expected. This one, however, was a special one as it reads this: **"Wish you a good journey"**. So this, I acknowledge, was the pivotal moment for me, in deciding that I needed to make this my good journey; to use it for the good of the lessons that I was being entrusted with, and I had this deep sense of knowing in my soul that this is "My WHY".

A Radio Contest—May 2011

I received a call from a local radio station a couple of weeks before Mothers' Day in 2011. The person informed me that my name had been drawn along with others, from a contest box where I had submitted an entry. The caller asked if I would be able to participate in a contest on Mothers' Day weekend. It just happened that we were already committed to a weekend of spring cleanup at our summer camp. It had been such a long winter, and I was looking forward to opening up our camp that upcoming weekend. So, I asked if I could have a friend step in for me to participate in the contest. The person from the radio station agreed with the stipulation that if my friend won the contest, we would need to figure out how to share the prize.

I called Wanda, who has become a very sweet and supportive friend. Wanda is Kenzie's boyfriend's mom. When I called Wanda and explained my dilemma, she just laughed and said sure, she would be willing to go play this radio contest with 103 other contestants.

Mothers' Day weekend arrived and Bob and I headed to our camp as planned. As we were raking the yard, my cell phone rang; it was Wanda explaining that only 66 contestants checked in at the contest so her odds of winning were even better. She explained that the contest consisted of rolling a ping pong ball down a trough of water and landing it on or closest to a mark in a pit of sand. It was a contest of elimination and no actual skill was involved. I wished Wanda good luck and asked her to keep me posted. As time moved on, I continued to receive updates from Wanda. She called when there were 33 people left, then 21, 13, 8, and then finally there were 2 people left: Wanda and another woman. Wanda handed the phone to her friend Nicky to converse with me as it was Wanda's turn next.

I could hear the crowd in the background and the radio DJ announcing like this: "Alright everyone, Wanda is up and she is rolling her ping pong ball down the water troth". Then I heard the crowd groan and it was obvious that Wanda's turn did not go so well. To hear Wanda explain it, her ball landed in the sand but then rolled off the course. It was time for the other opponent to take her turn. Just as Wanda did, the woman's ball bounced off and out of the sandpit. They would now go into sudden death. Wanda was up first and successfully landed her ball in the pit of sand however, it was not a good roll as it landed away from the mark, off in the corner. The other woman took her turn and rolled the ball and landed it exactly on the mark in the pit of sand. The crowd was cheering, and all of a sudden the ball swished right off the course. Wanda could only explain it this way: it was as if something just batted the ball off the course. Wanda won!!!! I won!!! An all-inclusive trip to Barbados!! We decided to go in February on Super Bowl Sunday as and actually the Patriots were in the Super Bowl playing New York. We had thought it would be fun, even though we would be leaving our husbands at home, to watch the game when we arrived at the resort. Wanda insists that this was Makenzie's Mothers' Day gift for Wanda and I and I believe that she is right.

Barbados—February 2012

The trip to Barbados was not uneventful. It was Super Bowl Sunday and the Pats were playing the Giants. We had hopes of watching the game at our destination. We started out with airplane mechanical issues and were removed from our original flight. The airline had no other flight that day and had to find seats for all the passengers on other commercial flights to get us to our destination. We were given seats on another airline to Miami and then on to Barbados after a very long lay over in Miami. The flight from Miami to Barbados was full. Wanda and I were not seated near each other. I had the privilege of sitting next to a very nice retired school teacher from Kansas. We chatted with each other the entire flight. As I shared with her the reason for our trip, along with many of the little signs that I felt my daughter was giving me, she commented that she felt like she was sitting next to the mother of her daughter's high school best friend. This woman explained that her daughter had a best friend name Brandy, who died when she was 17. She explained to me that some of the things that I was sharing with her seemed similar to things that this other mom had experienced after she lost her 17 year old daughter. She told me that the woman had even written a book co-authored with her pastor. I asked her to write down her friend's name as well as the name of her book. The book is called, Love Never Ends. I made a mental note that I would purchase the book and try to find this other mom with similar circumstances.

We arrived very late in Barbados. As we waited to go through customs, I remember stealing a look at the guard's TV; New York was winning. A driver picked us up and drove us on all sorts of back roads to get to the resort. It almost seemed like something out of the **Twilight Zone** as we drove very fast down these narrow roads with tall sugarcane crops aligning both sides of the road. Wanda and I kept quiet for the ride but shot each other several glances of uncertainty.

We arrived at the resort in the wee hours of the morning and were brought to our room, where we easily crashed into our beds and fell fast asleep. In the morning, I remember waking to the sounds of birds and almost like jungle sounds of bugs humming and the ocean waves crashing. Wanda said I think we have ocean out our slider door. I jumped out of bed and sure enough we had an oceanfront room. Below, and in front of us, were the beach and the ocean, and lots of unusual looking plants and trees. We got dressed and made our way down to breakfast and then to an introduction meeting to inform us of all the amenities and things to do. We decided to sign up for several of the excursions including one to an outside club which we were told was one that we did not want to miss! It included dinner and a show; this would turn out to be Wanda's nemesis.

On the beach in Barbados, we were frequently visited at our lounge chairs by natives who were selling their wares or services. I purchased a bird feeder made out of a coconut that was carved in the shape of a humming bird. There were a few people set up selling jewelry and t shirts. Wanda and I also made an appointment to get our hair braided. Oh, the things you decide to do while on vacation. Ha ha. Anyway, this one young kid came up to us, (his name was Lex), and was trying to get us to sign up for his private boat that would take us out to swim with the giant turtles. This would happen on Thursday. Although we were quite interested, the feeling of going on a private boat was unsettling. For all we knew, we might never come back. Every day he would stop by our chairs on the beach and remind us about it and encourage us to sign up. We finally did.

When Thursday came and we showed up where he told us to wait, he was there wearing a special T shirt. I said to Wanda, "Look at his T shirt". It was a T-shirt with the number 10 on it; (Kenzie's number 10), and it was black and white!. This was affirmation for me that everything was going to be alright. We took our pictures with Lex and his number 10 T-shirt. There were six of us on the boat as well as the crew. Wanda and I had no intention of swimming with the giant turtles. Instead, we thought we would just watch. As the other guests geared up with their life jackets and snorkels, one lady said to me that this was something I did not want to miss out on; that we really should just gear up. The thought of swimming around with these giant turtles that surrounded our little boat made me nervous. I did not know what to expect, nor did I want to swim in their poo. Wanda and I decided to put those feelings aside and we jumped in. What an amazing thing to do! The crew was feeding these creatures fish to keep them around the boat as we treaded water and touched them, sometimes even pushing them away as they surrounded us. The turtles were bigger than us and at times overwhelming. This was an amazing experience!

One of the excursions we took was to learn about the history of the island. There is both wealth and poverty on this island with both intermingled. We were taken to a beautiful church and a wild life sanctuary where we fed little green monkeys. When walking through this jungle of plants, one would not even know that these little monkeys were there watching and waiting. The park attendant fed these little monkeys at a certain time and they came out by the multitudes. We were surrounded by little green monkeys, and it too, had a feeling of uncertainty. You did not dare to walk because they were all around us. We stood frozen, watching.

Wanda and I had a wonderful vacation at the resort; we were welcomed each morning by waking up to the sounds of the ocean and tropical birds. We went on a few excursions offsite of the resort to get to know a little more about the island. One of our excursions was a rum tasting tour to Mount Gay Rum. It was very early in the morning to start drinking rum punch, but we managed. When we went into the bathroom the walls were covered with ceramic tiles that had the initials MG. We had to take a picture as one would almost think that Makenzie Goode was up to her tricks but, yes, another God wink.

Another excursion was to a local dive to experience a party band and show. The show consisted of fire dancers on stilts wearing masks and bright costumes. We were served dinner before the show. I had the beef, and Wanda chose the chicken. (My thought now is never choose the chicken in a foreign country). Although we certainly had a blast at this dive bar with the party band, Wanda suffered immensely a few days later. She had flu like symptoms and stayed in our room for the last couple days of our vacation. She suffered from fever, nausea, chills, etc. She was one sick girl. I actually went to the medical office at the resort and summoned a nurse to come check on her. Unfortunately, the resort was very limited in what they had to offer for over-the-counter remedies for flu like symptoms. Finally on Sunday morning, the day we were scheduled to leave, Wanda said to me that there was no way she was getting on that flight back to the States unless she felt better.

The Lady in Lavender

I decided to venture into town to see if I could find a pharmacy and get her something to help her feel better. I was told that if I followed the beach into town, I would find a pharmacy. I headed that way and passed rum shack after rum shack. I heard the church bells ringing. In Barbados, there is no division in classes. You will see a run-down shack for a home next to a very beautiful home or mansion. There are rum shacks at practically every corner, and usually right next to a church. One of our tour guides had made a funny remark that if you didn't find the spirit in one, you could certainly catch it in the other. Well, I found the pharmacy however, it was closed. The sign indicated that it would be open at 8am so I decided to wait the 15 minutes until it opened. While I stood there and waited, there were some local guys standing across the street drinking at a rum shack. One of the guys came over to me and asked me for some money. I was feeling very shaky as I told him that I really didn't have any money to give him. Just then, I heard my daughter's voice in my head. I heard her say, "Don't worry mom, I'll take care of you". I thought, "Wow, Kenzie, if you are really here with me and plan to protect me, you need to give me a bigger sign"! In my mind, I spoke those words to her. Immediately, an old Baja woman with very dark leathery skin came walking across the street. She was dressed to the hilt in a beautiful lavender dress and lavender picture hat. She came and stood with me. I complemented her dress and asked her about her jewelry. She had a picture of a young guy on a pin attached to the lapel of her dress jacket. She smiled a sad smile and explained to me that that was a picture of her son who she had lost a couple of years ago and that she was missing him pretty bad. Oh my goodness! That was my sign! Lavender was my daughter's favorite color and then the picture of the woman's deceased son. I told her that I was sorry. No other words were exchanged as the store opened up and she disappeared inside.

Love Never Ends

After returning from our trip, I felt the urgency to learn more about the author of the book, Connie Martin, after my "chance" encounter on the plane with her friend. The woman on the plane was from Kansas and she had explained to me that she thought that I could purchase the book on Amazon. I first tried that, but must not have been searching correctly as I had no luck. I then did some other searches on my computer and came upon an article about a book that had been co-authored by Connie and the pastor of her church. The article named the church in Kansas and as I did further investigation, I found the church and its phone number. I picked up the phone and called the pastor. After explaining my unusual connection with the woman from his congregation who wrote the book, he excitedly offered to take my information and share it with Connie.

Connie and I have become good friends. We share the same tragedy with different circumstances but, have the blessed assurance that our daughters are in heaven. We laugh as we agree that the girls have surely become friends as they continue to be up to their mischief even now, and how they must be delighting as their moms' are finding the treasures. Connie's unusual story, like mine, offers hope. There are so many similarities in the things that we stumble upon that show us that our daughters continue to be in our lives. I can see how Connie and I have been connected; our lives perfectly aligned for His purpose. Retrospectively, I notice things. I had placed a bench at the lake inscribed with our daughter's favorite scripture from 1Corinthians. The last three words are "Love Never Ends", (the title of Connie's book).

Interestingly enough, I also have been given the gift of a pastor to assist me in polishing my prose. I thank God every day for Pastor Rick. He is a humble and inspired servant of God.

May 2013- Kenzie's Birthday Weekend and **The Tree of Life**

Yesterday was such a wonderful day, as I tooled around the scenic coast of Ryc with friends Betty Ann and Jeffrey. We had several reminders that Makenzie was joining us throughout the day, and then this:

The Tree of Life

Our travel included a detour into Portsmouth so Betty could hit the fabric shop. (Betty Ann is a quilter, so I knew this wasn't a quick stop! ha ha). I ventured off on my own to hit the little shops on one of the side streets and wound up in a trendy upscale gift and home furnishings shop called "Wanderlust". I spoke briefly with the young girl cashier and started looking around. When I got to the back of the shop I came across a semi-empty shelf. On one side, there were a couple of pretty ornamental vases, and on the other side was a small piece of purple paper. It was a note. I picked up the note and there was a heart drawn on it with these words, "Keep Calm Cuz I Love You Mom". Really?! I snatched up the note and went to the cashier and asked the girl why that note was on that shelf. She kind of looked funny at me, so I explained to her about losing Kenz, and that it was her birthday weekend, and of all the little reminders that I receive. She got teary-eyed and said, "You know you need to have this". She said that maybe her mother had left it there on the shelf, she wasn't certain, and gave no other explanation.

Soon after, her mom joined us at the register and the girl introduced me and I shared so much more of my journey. I talked about the trip we had won to Barbados and about the lady with the lavender hat. Her mother smiled and took the piece of purple paper from me and placed it in a little plastic bag for me and said: "You realize that this note is for you, you have to have it". I shook my head in agreement. She then went over to the side of the shop and picked up something and brought it back to me. It was a necklace with a gold circle with a tree, and it had pretty little purple gem stones adorning the tree. She told me it was the Tree of Life and that she wanted me to have it. I burst into tears and told her she didn't realize what she had just given me. I explained that Barbados is known for the Tree of Life. There is a sign next to a very old tree in Barbados which says Tree of Life, Evergreen Conifer Oriental Thuja Platycladus Orientalis, 150 years old "circa". It is the custom there, that if you hug the tree you will add years to your life. I shared a bit about my trip to Barbados and of how my friend Wanda and I each hugged that Tree of Life.

Wanda in Barbados next to The Tree of Life

Liz W., the shop owner, was amazed as she was not aware that there really is a Tree of Life, nor of its location. With this gift, she gave me a tiny card that the artist had created to go with the necklace. This is what the card says:

The Tree of Life is symbolically described in the Book of Revelations as having curing properties

> *And he showed me a pure river of water of life, clear as crystal, proceeding from the throne of God and of the Lamb. In the middle of its street, and on either side of the river, was the tree of life, which bore twelve fruits, each tree yielding its fruit every month. The leaves of the tree were for the healing of the nations. Revelations 22:1-2.*

The little purple note that I discovered on Kenzie's Birthday weekend and the Tree of Life necklace

Another Wink

During the holidays of 2013, Bob found himself on the porch of Mim's Market. Mim's is a small little country store where people gather for a cup of coffee and a chat. Bob ran into our sweet friend Pam and stood there and gabbed for a bit. A man approached them while they were standing on the porch and he carried a large piece of art. He was trying to sell this very large piece of art and showed it to them. It is made of steel and is oval in shape and has the tree of life cut out in design. Bob and Pam shot each other a knowing look and Pam smiled and said, "I think that Makenzie is suggesting this for your Christmas gift to Marcy". Of course he made the purchase and wrapped it up and put it as best he could, under our Christmas tree. To me, it almost looked like the shape of one of those flying saucers that kids use for snow sledding. I was genuinely surprised and delighted to open this beautiful Tree of Life artwork. Bob recently finished it for me with a copper look finish and it hangs in our hallway.

Chapter Five

Scholarship and NEOB

For the first and second year anniversary dates we shared time together up at Pilgrim Pines. It was a small gathering of just her closest friends. The kids played broom ball and ice skated and played some board games inside. We had a light supper together and had a candlelight ceremony around a campfire on the beach to celebrate Makenzie's life. It was really nice to get together with her friends and I sensed that they needed to get together as well. After the second year, I felt like it would be difficult to get everyone together on the anniversary date, as so many had moved away and were attending colleges in different parts of the country. I also just felt that we needed to do something more on the positive side as Makenzie was so much the life of the party. We decided to start a Memorial Soccer Tournament in her name and it is held on the weekend following Christmas each year. This is not only to honor her memory but to also serve as the one fundraising event that I believe will continue annually. Everyone seems to enjoy this fun time celebrating the sport that my daughter loved so much. The funds raised go towards her memorial scholarship fund.

Team Thunder Buddies and Team PV Alumni 1

Team Farquad's Fury and Team Sunny Busters

The Makenzie Goode Memorial Scholarship Fund

My friend called me a day or so after we lost our girl, to suggest that I may want to consider establishing a scholarship in Makenzie's memory, in lieu of receiving far too many flowers for her services. I had actually considered the thought but was very grateful that Nancy H. called and put me in touch with the Community Foundation of North Central Mass. I needed guidance and there she was. I recognized that God was helping me fit the pieces together. I met with an attorney from the foundation, who guided me through the process of setting up the legal parameters of the scholarship. It was decided that the scholarship would be awarded to a graduating senior from Makenzie's high school. The recipient would be one who was furthering their education in either a sports related career or medicine, such as physical education, physical therapy, or nursing, etc. The scholarship recipient would have participated in varsity sports, with soccer taking first priority. Each applicant was asked to submit an essay written about how they had helped someone, an organization, or a cause. They were asked to state what they learned, as well as how the benefactor may have benefited from their contribution. There was an exception made that first year, with Makenzie's graduating class, and several scholarships were awarded to all of her graduating friends on the girls' soccer team.

My friend Nancy explained to me that fundraising early on would be important, and that acquiring a goal of around $20,000 would help it to become self-sustaining, perpetual, as the money was placed in a long-term investment fund. I decided to make that my goal.

Fundraising and more fundraising:

Fund-raising began immediately starting with the lavender t-shirts created by her friends at the school. Also, wrist bands were sold by the kids. I believe this gave them a positive avenue as they processed their grief. In the springtime for at least two years, the kids performed music in a talent show known as the Calliope Café, with the funds raised going to the scholarship fund. I am amazed at the creativity and generosity of so many people supporting this cause which was emotionally supporting me in the process. I received a text in July of 2013 from Sydney M. and would like to share it here:

Hey Marcy I'm one of the captains for the girls soccer team and we are planning on having a coin drop this Saturday in Northfield, and we were planning on donating 50% of our profits to the Kenzie scholarship fund if that's okay with you, thank you! I replied to her how wonderful and thanked her. Following the coin drop I received another text:

Hey my friend who is the other caption, Nicole B, and I just tried to get hold of you to let you know how we did with the coin drop. We wanted you to know that we made $621.07 for both the soccer team and the scholarship fund. We would love to meet you somewhere soon to give you the money if that's okay with you.

A time was made and I met with these two beautiful young girls who never really truly got to know my daughter but had occasion to interact with her in a small way on the soccer field during practices. These girls were younger and explained to me that Makenzie helped them during drills. I shared with them the scrap book that I was creating, that was keeping me going with all the positivity that I was experiencing during this my journey. Sydney and Nicole are really sweet girls. When it came time for them to turn over a portion of the profits from the coin drop they told me that the team got together and it was decided that they would donate all of the funds raised to the scholarship fund. They said they really did not need warm up jackets that badly. (Their original plan was to raise funds to help pay for new warm up jackets for the team). I see amazing empathy demonstrated by so many.

My friend Betty created and donated two beautiful quilts to raffle. Tickets were sold for several months with the winner picked at the school's fall homecoming. We also sold tickets for a "120 Club" and names were drawn weekly for cash prizes. One of Makenzie's besties, Casey, sold many tickets for this endeavor. The winning ticket was drawn at a Girls Varsity Basketball game, and to our delight, Casey's ticket was randomly drawn in front of the crowd for the top prize of $500.00. Casey wanted to donate the money back to benefit the Scholarship Fund. However, we felt it appropriate that she keep the prize money as her name was picked. I believe that somehow my daughter had something to do with Casey's winning ticket being picked out of so many. Casey was attending college and certainly could use additional finances.

More fundraising included a bottle tree. Bob created a beautiful lighted bottle tree for our summer camp and also made one to raffle. We also had two beautiful glass beads created by a local artist, Ericka M. They fit Pandora style bracelets and are beautiful. One is lavender with intricate flowers and the other is lavender with zebra stripes. I became a "professional" vendor at all sorts of events. There were Old Home Days, and fall festivals, holiday fairs, and even an oyster festival. I sat there for eight hours a day and many times had the assistance and company of my sister, my friend Wanda, Brenda T., Stormie, and some of Kenzie's friends, and of course, Bob, who never let me out of his sight for long. It was very emotional sitting there with a sign and a picture of my daughter, hoping that people would contribute to her memory for her memorial scholarship fund. People are for the most part, kind, compassionate, and charitable. I cannot tell you how many hugs I received. This fundraising provided a form of therapy for me as I shared her story. I found that God placed just the right people in my path at exactly the time that I needed them.

Blessed be the God our Father and the Lord Jesus Christ, the Father of mercies and the God of all comfort; who comforts us in all our affliction so that we may be able to comfort those wo are in any affliction with the comfort with which we ourselves are comforted by God. 2 Corinthians 1:3-4

I remember my friend Kim had given me a bin filled with Beanie Baby stuffed animals to sell at one of my many fundraising events. This particular event was not going so well. It was a pumpkin festival where people were celebrating with their children and would simply walk right by me. Many times people did not know how to interact with me and simply would not make eye contact. I was feeling sad and asked God to place someone special in my path. God delivered a very nice woman who purchased almost all of the Beanie Babies for her little granddaughters. I got a kick out of watching these little girls select these stuffed animals out of the bin. The woman was so kind in supporting me and the scholarship in this way.

By the fifth year anniversary of Kenzie's death, we had accomplished our goal of $20,000 even after paying out 19 scholarships by year five.

NEOB Volunteer

I became involved with New England Organ Bank and Donate Life early on. I needed to be involved in something meaningful. First they offered me a volunteer position as their Registry Ambassador to visit the local RMV monthly to remind the workers of the importance of encouraging MA drivers to register for organ and tissue donation. Although my stint at this was short lived, I have to say I met wonderful workers who truly engaged with me as I shared Makenzie's story. Volunteering in this capacity just did not seem to be the right fit for me. I felt that I needed broader interaction to get Makenzie's story out.

Next, I served at a few Donor Registration tables/booths to encourage registration. We worked at several colleges to meet the kids and discuss our plight. For the most part, I found the individuals that I spoke with were already registered. I met a young girl named K. who volunteered with me at Mt. Holyoke College. She was a recipient of a liver a couple of years earlier and as she explained, before she received her gift of life, she was one very ill young college girl. This was certainly a life event for her. Our conversation was interesting and she shared a fun little story. I asked her if she had experienced anything unusual post-transplant and she said yes. She explained that although she was not much of a TV watcher, she was now drawn to a show called "Say Yes to the Dress". She hadn't wanted to miss an episode. The show was about fashion and making each bride's experience unforgettable, going sometimes to extreme lengths to help each bride realize her dreams. K. explained to me that she had the opportunity to correspond with her donor family and learned that her donor was a woman in her seventies who created bridal gowns all her life. It's interesting that K. now had an affinity for this show.

I met my friend Robin and her supportive friend Lacy at a New England Organ Bank Volunteer Recognition Banquet. We became fast friends as I shared stories of my communication with Kenzie's recipients. Robin is so hopeful to meet her donor family one day and to be able to personally thank them for their life saving gift. Unfortunately, like so many other donor families, they find it difficult and some are never able to make this connection. As I was leaving the event, Robin asked me if she could find me on social media and I agreed and we exchanged names. After I wrote my name down she smiled and laughed and said," O.K. wait till you read my name". I had written Marcy Robitaille and she wrote her name down for me. Her name is Robin Lataille. Hmmm, I think that we were destined to meet.

Robin has such a commitment to fostering awareness of organ and tissue donation. She is a swimmer for Team USA and has competed in three World Games; Sweden, Africa and Argentina. She has won several gold and silver medals. She was insisting that I should join her in the Games, as recently she also became involved in the Transplant Games of America. These games occur bi-annually and have thus taken place in Grand Rapids, Michigan and Houston with the upcoming 2016 games planned for Cleveland.

I had the pleasure of joining Team New England in Houston, TX in July 2014. What a wonderful event. Six thousand people joined in to compete in all sorts of events which included swimming, basketball, volleyball, golf, badminton, ballroom dancing, bowling, poker, softball, and even a 5K walk/run marathon event. One of the highlights was trading pins. Team New England provided each of us with a bag of pins. They were designed as lighthouse pins that say Team New England. Each team had unique pins created to represent their home state. We exchanged pins throughout the weekend trying to collect as many other states represented as possible. I was fortunate to get Hawaii's pin as they had a very small team represented; only a few people attended. Puerto Rico was a hot commodity as they only had three team members as well and thus ran out of pins quickly. The pins were cute; Indiana had a race car, and Arizona had an Alien. Texas had a State of Texas with two spurs dangling from it. California had a surf board. I had fun as I competed with Robin to get more states than her. Robin is so very competitive!

The Opening Games were incredible. They lined up the teams by each state represented, in alphabetical order so that we could march into the stadium. I was invited to march in with our team athletes carrying the Donate Life banner with a few other donor family members. I feel blessed to have met these other donor families as we share a common bond. As we marched into the stadium, the announcer announced fun facts about the team; the youngest athlete on our team, a 10 year old heart recipient and also announcing the oldest on the team, an 84 year old man. The music was invigorating including the theme from the movie Rocky. After the athletes marched in, the next group was the supporters and extended families of the recipients. As they came in, the other donor family friends and me, headed to the back of the stadium to come back through the tunnel. This is the same tunnel that the football players run through at a professional football game. We had a long wait in the tunnel and I got to know a woman and her husband as she shared her immense loss. She told me how her son had taken his life only a couple of months after we lost Makenzie. His name was CJ and he was only 20 years old. I fully understood the pain and guilt this woman was sharing with me, but I sensed that unlike me, she had not found hope.

She explained to me that she did not believe in heaven or hell and had no belief in God. This really affected me. I spent the following thirty or so minutes trying to share my faith in Christ and the hope and peace that I have, knowing that I will see my daughter again. I encouraged her to find a church and she simply asked "Why"? My simple answer was that what she was doing did not seem to bring her hope. (She did not have joy that was apparent to me). She seemed so very sad and had a numb, complacent affect. She did not share in the joy and peace that I have come to depend on in my life now. We did share the fact that we need to stay busy and always focused on the next thing to help move us forward.

Hallie and her husband are involved in many fundraising events in their son's memory and are definitely paying it forward. Hallie even gifted one of her own kidneys to a perfect stranger. To me, that is amazing and she is making her ripple in life. They started a website entitled "Scattering CJ". She explained to me that her son loved adventure in life and would have wanted to see the world. I will explain a bit more, later.

Anyway, after Hallie and I shared, we exited the football tunnel along with the other donor family representatives and marched into the huge stadium. The crowds in the audience stood and cheered. Each donor family carried a special memento of their loved one, whether it was a picture, stuffed animal, a trophy, anything that was a special item to remember their loved one. I carried the little stuffed zebra that I had given to Makenzie in her last Easter basket. That zebra mascot rode around with her in the rear window of her Grand Am and was with her when she had her accident. It is a white zebra with black stripes. I also carried a sign that says "Life is Good". I was wearing the traveling t-shirt. It was a very emotional event as we made our way around the stadium and waved to the crowd. People in the front rows were reaching out and shaking our hands if we would take them and yelling, "Thank you", "Thank you", and "God Bless You". I found tears streaming down my cheeks when I thought that I could not cry anymore. I want to be sure that it is understood, as you read this, that this was for Makenzie. This was her accolade. I like to believe that she had a heavenly view of all of this and realized how very proud her mom is of her.

The guest entertainer at the opening games was Scott MacIntyre, eighth place finalist on the eighth season of American Idol. He is a pianist and songwriter. Scott is legally blind and has suffered from end stage kidney disease. He has had two kidney transplants. He was a great addition to the opening ceremonies.

One of the events that we participated in, at the Games, was a Quilt Pinning event. We were invited to create a quilt square to represent our loved one. My friend Betty created a beautiful square with soccer ball fabric and zebra stripes, embroidered with Makenzie's name and the words "Life is Goode". As we entered the hall where the Quilt Pinning was to take place, I was amazed at the already completed quilts that graced the room. There were so many beautiful quilts, each square telling a story of its own. The squares displayed the donor's names, pictures, and hobbies, to represent their beautiful lives. There were three completed quilts of just police badges. After the loss of a fallen police officer, the father of that officer decided to learn how to sew and quilt. I believe he was in his seventies, and his mission was to create quilt squares each displaying a badge from police departments around the country. These blue, gold and white badges make beautiful quilts.

The ceremony of the quilt pinning provided each of us an opportunity to stand in front of the room and say something about our loved one. We then pinned our square on a blank quilt where the square will eventually be permanently affixed. Our quilts from the 2014 Transplant Games of America will be on display at all future games.

There was a special Donor Recognition Ceremony held at the Wortham Theater Center in downtown Houston. Special signs with our loved one's picture were there, placed on easels lined up row after row after row. I felt the heaviness in the air when I arrived. This was going to be a solemn occasion. I decided to look for Makenzie's sign and as I walked from easel to easel, row after row, a tearful woman noticed me and grabbed my hand. She said, "You must be looking for your daughter, she's over here! I saw her and she looks just like you". Makenzie's sign said in bold letters: "Kenzie, Because of You, Life is Goode". That's when I lost it. It is times like this that reality sneaks up and stings you. The donor ceremony was held in a large theater with some selected guest speakers. There was a power point presentation accompanied by music. Each of our lost loved ones was represented in the presentation. It was a sad but meaningful ceremony.

Sign at the Donor Recognition Ceremony

Interaction with so many beautiful people during our time at The Transplant Games of America was wonderful. I received many random hugs as people saw my Donor Family Badge. They would cross the length of a hallway just to meet me. Their stories truly inspired me as they too, suffered immeasurably in life but, received a second chance. Most of the people that I had the pleasure of meeting, are giving back in life. What a blessing to be able to do just that.

Team New England of Donate Life /New England Organ Bank

Scattering CJ

Meeting Hallie and her husband at the Transplant Games was no coincidence. Again, I feel it was His divine purpose being realized. After CJ's death, Hallie and her husband established a website where people could read and comment on the amazing stories of where CJ's ashes were being scattered. Because their son was full of adventure, they felt he would have traveled the world in his life, had it not ended. They offered to allow people to take a small amount of CJ's ashes, (quarter size), and scatter them around the world. They received over 6000 requests to participate in this endeavor. I, too, was granted the privilege of scattering some of CJ. Here is the letter that I wrote to CJ's parents.

November 2014
Dear Hallie and John,

> *Yesterday was a lovely day and made more beautiful by remembering your sweet boy. I think it inspiring that you and I have met under such sad circumstances. Both our kids have left us way too early, but have shared their lives with others and have given back and made their ripple in*

life. I took Makenzie's picture alongside of CJ's, because we were taking the journey back to one of her favorite places. Although it is not in some famous or far and distant land, for our family, this place is one of the happiest places on earth. I thought that I would share some of the wonderful memories that we shared, so you can understand why I chose each spot.

I decided that bringing CJ up to Kenzie's memorial bench would be a nice place to start. The bench overlooks the frog pond and also the lake where we as a family have had so much fun. I remember countless hours with our kids knee-deep in mucky muck trying to catch the biggest bullfrog for the weekly frog jumping contest that they held at family camp. Ahhh, those are really great memories. So it seemed like a really happy place to scatter some of CJ as the frog catching tradition carries on even now with our grandson. I also spread some of his ashes at her bench. We placed a plaque there with her favorite Bible verse: 1 Corinthians 13:4-7. I hope you will find it as meaningful as we do.

"Love is patient; love is kind; love is not envious or boastful or arrogant or rude. It does not insist on its own way; it is not irritable or resentful; it does not rejoice in wrongdoing, but rejoices in the truth. It bears all things, believes all things, endures all things. <u>Love never ends</u>". 1 Corinthians 13:4-8 New Revised Standard Version (NRSV)

Next I decided to take a walk up on the camp roads where our family camped. I headed to this quiet little secluded pond in the back of the campsites where the kids would try to catch a fish. There is a bench that sits overlooking the pond and I remember many early mornings heading there with my cup of coffee to sit and reflect. This spot seemed like a really nice place to leave some of CJ. It is one of God's perfect settings in New Hampshire. I lit a candle there and told CJ how much his family loved him. As I sat on that bench, I remember thinking about the walks around the camp roads with my children.

We used to like to walk at night with our lantern and flashlights and pass by the other campsites to see what everyone was doing. There were card games being played, and laughter around campfires, sometimes guitars and singing as well. Families were just enjoying each other and being thankful for time together. I will never forget one of those walks that I had with Makenzie. She was only about nine or ten years old. She had just attended youth Camp, the bible camp up the road, the previous week, and she had returned to us to finish up the weekend with us at the campground. As we took our lantern-lit walk on the camp roads, she asked me if I believed in angels. I remember saying that I did and asking her why did she ask. She explained that the night before at Bible camp, when they held their end of the week campfire, she saw an angel sitting on the big rock and it was glowing.

I smile at this memory and so, decided that this would be a place I would need to take CJ. I headed up the road to the youth camp, to the place in the woods where they have their ceremonial end of week campfire. It was so very quiet to be walking through the camp in November with not a soul around, but it was a very peace-filled quiet. I was happy to see a wooden cross hanging above the campfire pit. I tried to imagine where my daughter had been seated when she saw the angel sitting on the big rock.

Kenzie's Angel Rock-Scattering CJ

It seemed important to light the candle in the fire pit and to say a prayer for CJ. I asked God to forgive CJ for giving up on life and prayed that God would take care of him in heaven. I thought it would be nice to scatter some of CJ's ashes on top of the big rock where Makenzie saw the angel.

Hallie, I want you to know how meaningful this youth camp has been to me in my life. I used to attend this same camp when I was just a kid; every summer pleading with my folks to let me stay just one more week. One of my most meaningful experiences was at the Camp's end of the week campfire. That particular week it was a smaller camp than usual. Instead of holding the campfire at the traditional spot with the big rock, they held it down by the lakeside. The counselors handed out to each of us a candle and we stood in a circle to pass the flame from one to another. We were asked to comment on something we would like to ask God to help us with such as like selfishness, dishonesty, sadness, greed, conceit, etc., as we passed the flame to the next person. After all the candles were lit, we placed our candles in a large wooden cross. The cross was lying on the ground by the lakeside and it had holes drilled in it where we could place our lit candles. After all the candles were placed in the cross, a couple of the counselors towed the cross out further in the water, a bit off shore, with a rowboat. It was beautiful and this left such a lasting impression on me.

My next journey with CJ was to go down to the lakeside. My sweet friend Wanda had given me a zebra-painted cross in memory of my daughter and it seemed perfect to bring it down there and place it on the shore. Hallie, I lit the candle for you this time. I asked God to take away your guilt and your grief and prayed that somehow you would find the peace that only He through His son, Jesus, can offer, and that you might find joy in the days ahead until you see your CJ again. The lake is so beautiful and such a happy place. I felt it would be perfect to scatter some of CJ here where I prayed for you.

*After this, I headed back up the hill to the main road as I had one more place to go. When I got to the top of the road I had to smile the biggest smile as I was shown a little gift. In the window of one of the cabins, someone had painted in purple paint (Kenzie's favorite color) these words: "**Life is good**". Makenzie's last name was Goode, and I see these words often. It is usually when I am feeling inspired by her,*

My last stop was to head to the beach. The beach in the summer months has so much activity and is the meeting place for everything. The snack shack is there, the canoes and kayaks are there, the water slide and inflatable "blob" are there, as well as a dock. There

Zebra cross at lake-side-Scattering CJ

is a basketball court, play-ground, and volleyball net too; just the hub of all the family fun of family camp. Walking onto the beach I saw two beautiful ducks gliding through the water and it made me wonder if CJ and Makenzie have met. Your description of your son reminded me so much of Kenzie. She too was happy, loved her family, and was always the life of the party. As you requested, I reminded CJ

Life is Good painted cabin window-A God Wink for sure

again that you loved him and that you were sorry. I drew a big heart in the sand and placed the last of his ashes in the "o" of the word love. It is supposed to snow tomorrow so I will imagine that the snow will cover this message, to keep it frozen in time until the next family camping time approaches.

Thank you for this honor, Hallie and John, for giving me the opportunity to not only honor and remember your son but to take this walk around our beloved camp and to remember such cherished memories.

Your friend,
Marcy

The spreading of CJ's ashes reminded me of our own traveling T-shirt. Immediately following Kenzie's tragedy, the kids at school had a lavender t-shirt made up with her picture and a zebra-striped number 10 on the back. They sold the t-shirt as a fundraiser for the scholarship fund; a measure designed to turn this tragedy into something more positive. Thank you, Cody R. for spearheading this! The Traveling T-shirt is a means for friends and family to take Makenzie with them as they travel to far and distant places. I have received pictures of her friends wearing the t-shirt in places like Ecuador, Italy, Barbados, Florida Panhandle, Alaska, Nova Scotia, the Grand Canyon, Hawaii, Athens Greece, New Zealand, and even to the peak of Mt. Kilimanjaro. I wanted to share a text message that I received on the anniversary date from our sweet Yona while she was traveling in New Zealand. Yona is Kayla's little sis and so Makenzie's "adopted" little sister.

Hi Marcy! I just woke up here in New Zealand (6am on the 31st) but I can't forget what day it is back home! I know everyone is sending their love today and that is an amazing but hard thing. I will obviously be thinking of Kenzie and you, and I also wanted to let you know that I will be bringing her with me onto a Maori! So here in New Zealand the native people have gathering lands that are sacred which are called Maoris. We are going first to Maori today and one of the traditions is to invite your whakapapa or your ancestors that have passed on. And to me, that is Kenzie and dad. So I just wanted to let you know that I will be honoring Kenzie and my dad together today! I love you so much Marcy and I'm not sure how this will end up today but I think if there is any time to try, it's today, a day that I can feel her strong presence with me. I love you again! And keep a smile on your beautiful face! I'm sure that's what Kenzie would want! And I know that's what I hope for you! I will let you know how today goes later on! Lots of love and a big hug!

Chapter Six

Remembering You

I visited PVRS (Kenzie's high school), in March 2014. I like to drop in on Colleen B., Makenzie's past guidance counselor, on occasion. On this particular day in March, I was feeling kind of down and don't actually know why, but I just decided to drop in on her. Colleen shared with me that a month ago, on the anniversary date, that somehow an English assignment of Makenzie's dated 01/28/2010 appeared on her desk with her report card. January 28, 2010 was the last day that Kenzie attended school. Colleen said she had no idea how that assignment got on her desk, nor how Kenzie's report card showed up as well. Interestingly enough, the assignment was a sonnet where Kenzie had to mark the rhyme scheme and divisions. This is the sonnet:

Remember me when I am gone away.
Gone far away into the silent land;
When you can no more hold me by the hand,

Nor I half turn to go yet turning stay.
Remember me when no more day by day

You tell me of our future that you planned:
Only remember me; you understand

It will be late to counsel then or pray.
Yet if you should forget me for a while

And afterwards remember, do not grieve:
For if the darkness and corruption leave

A vestige of the thoughts that once I had,
Better by far you should forget and smile

Than that you remember and be sad.
Christina Rossetti (1830-1894)

We Remember You

Kenz, I remember happiness on the day you were born. I heard the nurse say "Happy Birthday little girl". I said to your dad, "Shhhhhhhh. Did they say girl"? My happiest moment in life was the day you entered it.

What a cute little girl you were, and very, very shy at first. Nevertheless, that didn't last and no matter where I went, out and about, someone knew you. You were happy and made others happy. I remember when you got chicken pox at age 5 and I wanted to take yours and Lindsay's picture. (I said you girls will look back at this and laugh). But no, you were not having any part of that. I remember there was a time when you would not answer to any name but Pocahontas, so I relented. You were a shining star in school both academically and athletically. You played flute as a little girl and the instructor told me to keep you at it and that you were good, so good, that she thought you could become first chair symphony good. But, you gave it up. After gymnastics for a bit, you chose soccer and you put your heart into it. I remember what a defender you became not only on the field but in life as well. You defended the odd person out and even as a small child would jump to the defense of others.

I was so proud of you when you invited Lucas to your birthday party. Lucas has Downs Syndrome, and yet you befriended him and he became well-loved at school. His mom was so excited when he got the invitation and explained that Lucas had never been invited to a birthday party before. I love that you had such a compassionate spirit. Just yesterday, I was driving and passed a certain spot in town and remembered when you made me stop the car because there was an injured turtle trying to cross. You picked it up and brought it down to some water to help it.

I adored your fun loving spirit and most of all, those crazy goofy expressions. You and Alyssa would make distorted faces on the soccer field to try and psyche the opposing team out. I wonder what they thought. It doesn't matter as you were having fun at it. You would talk with foreign accents with Kayla and Danielle. I remember how much you enjoyed dressing up for Halloween, once as a giant pink flamingo and another time with an inflatable Chef Boyardee costume. You would purposely get knocked down in that inflatable costume, and roll around on the ground just for laughs. You also dressed up like zombies with Danielle and made so many movies with all of your friends just for fun.

When you were 15, you asked me if I would order mermaid suits for you and your friends so you could stand on the beach at Old Orchard and pretend to be mermaids. You were always the life of the party. You and Danielle dressed like pirates and pimped out the golf cart at the campground and drove around to music from Pirates of the Caribbean. You had a bumper sticker that said Pirate Chicks Rock. You would talk in Pirate lingo. You loved OOB (Old Orchard Beach). I hardly saw you as you spent so much time there with your second family.

Kenz, you had so much fun in school and had such amazing friends. I remember in junior high you went to your first school dance. When I picked you and your friends up, they said you were doing the worm. I scolded you. (You were wearing a dress, ha ha). There were so many trips to birthday parties, basketball games, soccer practice and more games, dances, and float building, and sleep overs. I am so grateful that I had the chance to be your chauffeur.

You loved camp, amazing summer camp, Camp Squanto. You and Kayla were so excited to get there early to get top bunks. Listening to the funny stories that your camp friends have shared with me since then, little did I know what my sweet princess was doing at Christian camp. I have to laugh as I see the glimmer in Kayla's eyes and her unending smile, as she shares with me the silly things that you did. When I would come to pick you up at the end of camp, you would mouth the words "not yet" accompanied by your big tears, not wanting to leave. I'm so glad that you had such a wonderful time.

Your brother and you had fun growing up. Living in such a quiet rural place you pretty much just had each other for most of the time. Sean would talk you into doing so many things; like climbing out your bedroom window and shimmying down a make-shift rope only to find that your dad was in the garage working right next to the window where you were shimmying. Your brother would make you stand in the middle of the driveway holding flags as he raced by you trying all sort of tricks on his bike. You would get knocked down but never let it get you down. You were such a good sister. You were your brother's biggest fan; so loyal, yet you had very high expectations and never caved when it came to doing what was right. You loved your family, especially your cousins. Paige and you were inseparable as little kids, enjoying so many sleepovers, and then bridesmaids at Jen's wedding. Always the center of attention, you fainted just as Jen and Phil were exchanging their vows. And you adored your cousin Jason, a similar jokester, making fun at our regular holiday gatherings. (Jason loves you so much that he and his wife Heather named his sweet baby girl after you). I remember when you tattooed your dad with kitty cat tattoos while he was napping. He never knew until the guys at work the next day asked him about the tattoos on his arm.

Your favorite pet was your cat named Leo. You liked the game mancala, a little game with colored stones. You loved all kinds of music. I still listen to your IPOD and think that you just had the greatest taste in music. You loved Shrek, all of the movies, and went each year as it opened on your birthday. And you liked the show Dinosaurs. "Not the mama. Not the mama." You and your brother would watch the movie Hocus Pocus and laugh when it came to the three witches getting their brooms out of the closet. One got stuck with a Hoover.

I remember your first and only car. You named it Romeo after the song Love Story by Taylor Swift. A beautiful little red Grand Am with awesome rims. When I saw it, I had to bring it to you for a test run. You were working at the nursing home that day and I surprised you. The look on your face when you saw the car told me you just had to have it. You also had to have zebra seat covers to go in it. Speaking of the nursing home reminds me of how nervous you were when you started that job. You said you were afraid of old people. That changed for you as you came home after each shift and shared so many funny stories. You had your favorites and I know the residents there adored you. Who wouldn't? You were always smiling, always happy.

I remember when Matt came to pick you up for your first date, I wanted to meet him. I shook his hand and exchanged maybe two words and that was enough for me. I knew you would be fine. Matt, like all of your friends, is exceptional. You had extraordinary friends Kenz, because that was who you were.

I wanted to get some of these memories down on paper so I won't forget. I hope that maybe your friends will add some fun memories here for me as well. We will always remember you; but I want to close this with this...

Lighting a candle for you Kenz, but the flame inside of me will never go out. You are my joy, my laughter, and my hope. It will be the greatest day when we meet again.

Danielle D.

Five years ago I lost my best friend in the entire world. I wanted to post something way earlier today but every time I sat down to try to write something I got too overwhelmed with emotions. Makenzie, not a day goes by that I don't think about you. Some days it still doesn't even feel real. I miss being able to call you at any hour of the night or day to tell you all my crazy stories or just ramble on the phone with you for hours and hours! I wish you were still around so you could come with me on my crazy adven-

Kenzie and BFF Danielle

tures. I miss writing songs with you. I miss dressing up and making movies or having a photoshoot with you! I miss going to Maine with you walking on the boardwalk, talking to strangers and making up weird stories while talking in strange accents! I miss jumping on the trampoline with you. I miss dancing with you. I miss how you used to walk around department stores acting like you were mentally challenged or insane. I even miss you eating all my candy!! We had so much fun together and made so many amazing memories. Nobody could put a smile on my face like you. You taught me so much in my life. You were never afraid to just be yourself, or to be spontaneous and do something crazy, and to love everyone and everything around you! You made everybody laugh and brought sunshine to everyone's day!!! I miss you more than anybody will ever know and I'm counting down the days 'til I see you again. I love you Kenzie

Brittney L.

I think when it comes to death, eventually you learn to accept and live on for them. Living every day to its fullest because others did not get that chance. That is exactly what you did. You lived everyday like it was your last. I have definitely learned from the best. Some of the chances I have taken in my life are inspirations from you. I can't believe it's been five years already. It seems like just yesterday we were on that field having the time of our lives. I will never forget everything that you taught me and I know that you have helped guide me to where I am today. Now I am living in Morocco, thinking about you every day and how much you would have loved this country. But I know you are here with me, enjoying every step of the way. Keep shining on girl, I know that you are guiding all of us.

Oceania B.

Reflecting upon this day and the past 5 years, it is still so amazing to me how time flies. And still I think of the 9 that unraveled since the last time I saw Kenzie Goode. So many changes have come around since then. I am so grateful that in all my time I was so lucky to know and love such a sweet person; truly a blessing. My heart goes out to Marcy and everyone missing Kenzie today.

Alyssa H.

I have spent all day trying to think of something to say, and looking through old pictures, reading old comments and messages, and thinking of all of the memories. I am reminded of how long it truly has been, and as I have said before sometimes if feels like it's been so long, and other times it feels like just yesterday. You touched so many people, and showed so many people love, and gave us the gift of memories to last a lifetime.

I've always been told you won't be called home until it's your time. I guess Heaven was in need of a hero...somebody just like you. When I try to make it make sense in my mind the only conclusion I come to is that Heaven was in need of a hero like you.

We love and miss you Kenzie. Forever, BTF, Living the Goode Life.

Vanessa T.

I remember exactly where I stood when my phone started ringing 5 years ago on that day. At the time I couldn't understand why or how (and I don't think I really ever will) but I know every day that you help your wonderful mother and all of your loving friends remember to live each day at 115%. Your spirit lives on in each of us. I love and miss you Kenzie.

Thank you for reminding me what life is truly all about. X

Danielle A.

Taking a minute to stop and think about your bright smile and all of the happy memories I had with you. You turned my whole day around and reminded me how I should be living. Thank you for being a sign of hope, joy, and happiness in the world.

Liza A.

Kenzie, your silly, fun-loving, generous spirit continues to live on every day, and I will always be inspired by your dance moves, contagious personality, and advice on the soccer field. Life is Goode. RIP

Meghan H.

Making today a Goode day in honor of our dearest and never forgotten friend Kenzie Goode. Your smile, charm and positive energy are a few of the things that always come to mind when I think of you; things that 5 years ago we never expected we would lose, but after time has passed I think we have all realized that we never actually lost these things as you have continued to live on in all of us. Each day you have reminded us to move forward with smiles on our faces, and we will continue to do just that because we love you, forever.

Kaylee J.

I wonder what new songs you would be obsessed with. I wonder what new inside jokes we would be making today. I wonder if you would be proud of who I've become and where I am going. I miss you Kenzie. Five years have passed and a lot has changed but I've learned that change is good and to not be afraid of anything. Thank you for being such a big part of my life and you will always continue to be. Life is Goode. Love you girl.

Chelsey M.

Kenzie, I will never understand the reason for the tragedy that took you from us 5 years ago, until the day I die and I can ask God why myself.

Without you, the world is a much less funnier and happy place. But you've shown us how precious each day of life is and I will carry your love and laughter with me ALWAYS. Shine down extra bright on your family today. I am so blessed to have been a part of your life – until we meet again.

#KenzieMiaGoode #foreveryoung

Good friends **Nick D.** and **Cody B**. dedicated this song and sang it at a variety type spring concert held at the school in April following her passing. There was not a dry eye in the place.

Kenzie's Song
How can I stop myself from this fear of falling?
It only takes one second to save your breathing
Please can you tell me, I'll listen if you are grounded
Then I can finally start to collect my pieces
If you swear it'll be ok can I believe you?
When I'm jealous of being a little bit younger
When reality wasn't so real to us
I could live without this emptiness
Is it selfish to say your name when I'm sleeping?
Or cover mountains of loneliness when I'm awake?
You can hear me and company when things feel like it's almost ok
For now I can't call it back till my mind goes to you
If you swear it'll be ok can I believe you?
When I'm jealous of being a little bit younger
When reality wasn't so real to us
I could live without this emptiness
*Lyrics by Cody Ball

The Fox

The morning of the 29th when we were up getting ready for the day, I stood at the kitchen window and saw in the field across the street a beautiful red fox trotting through the snow. I remember yelling out to Kenzie to hurry and look out her window at the fox in the field. She told me that she couldn't see it. Those were the last words that we spoke to each other.

Spirit Week-sophomore year

Sophomore Dinner Dance

Months after when I was having a conversation with my friend Maryann, she told me a story about her fox. This is Mary's story:

The year that my father died, (and no one suspected that that would happen), we had an over population of squirrels in our yard. Like, 28 fat squirrels in the back yard, 18 in the front yard. It was remarkable. My dad said that he was going to get a 22 rifle and put a chair out there, and sit and wait for them to come".

After a visit from my sister and her husband around Thanksgiving time, they had left us with some unripe pears. The pears had refused to ripen and so I put them out in the back yard thinking that they wouldn't go to waste because the squirrels will eat them. At that, my dad said "MaryAnn! You're not feeding those squirrels, are you"? He then explained, "The squirrels will destroy your house! They will get into the attic, they will make a mess, they will chew the wires, and they will cause a fire"! So that explained to me his need for a rifle.

On Dec.3rd, my dad woke me at dawn and requested that I make him a cup of tea and that I contact my siblings, other family members, and Natalie his girl. He was ill after experiencing months of a persistent cough and had undergone diagnostic testing. Later that day my dad received the Sacrament for the Sick and admitted that he should go to the hospital. After maybe six days in the hospital, my dad was sent home on hospice due to lymphoma.

At some point, my dad gave up on the idea of a rifle to deter the squirrels and stated that I was not to worry; that God would send something to take care of our population of squirrels.

On December 13th, my brother, who, with my sister, was staying in Dad's home with me while he was being cared for under Hospice, announced "Come See! There's a fox in the back yard." We looked out the kitchen windows to see a most beautiful fox in a patch of sunlight at the base of a maple, on a pile of leaves that had accumulated there. The fox circled and snuggled down. We got our dad's binoculars and looked at that beautiful creature. Now we had a fox to chase the squirrels. We told our dad and he nodded wisely. He was comforted by that knowledge. Later that afternoon, he died. At 4:30, the time that he usually attended mass.

After Mary shared her story with me, I wondered if it had any significance or just mere coincidence, and I have to wonder about the sign of a fox now. I see them apprehensively and wonder if there is imminent death around me. More recently I saw a fox in the early evening. I was riding with my husband on a back country road in our small town. I thought to myself, oh boy, there is another fox and remember that you saw this fox. The next day I learned about the death of a family friend. He was a young 50+ years and had fought kidney failure for a long portion of his life. He had received a kidney transplant within the past year. I learned that he had passed that evening around the same time that I had seen the fox.

Another recent sighting of a fox was on my way to work one morning and I had again the thought to pay attention, whose death would I learn of next? I was contacted by my close friend Pam that same day informing me of the death of a sixteen year old girl in our small town. Pam wondered if I would be willing to connect right away with the grieving mom. Of course I agreed to, although I felt it was too soon. That next evening Pam called me again to ask if I could stop what I was doing and go visit this grieving mom. We headed over and to my surprise, this mom, Denyse, wasn't a mess, as I suspected. We talked a long time about our girls and similarities in what had happened. Pam chimed in to say that it was amazing to see how parallel our lives were in many respects, and that both Denyse and I had articulated things to Pam at separate times, basically saying the very same thing, in the very same words. Both Denyse and I had this feeling all of our lives that we were going to lose our girls. I can't explain it, but for me, I had this fear and perhaps even a deep knowing that Makenzie would leave me at an early age.

I attended the memorial service for Denyse's daughter, Gabby, that following Sunday afternoon. It was a celebration of her life being held on our town common. I was pleased to see the loving support that this town of ours extended to Denyse as she was not a long time resident. There was opportunity to share about Gabby and what I learned from the stories shared was that she was a crazy girl; fun, energetic, and confident young girl much like my own Makenzie. I was in awe of how well Denyse held up. During the memorial, a prayer shawl was presented as a gift from a friend in town. It was purple just like the one given to me those years ago. The shawl was passed from person to person to say a prayer for Denyse and for Gabby. I was so happy to see this as I thought of my prayer shawl and the amazing gift that it was for me.

Afterwards I went up to the remembrance table to view pictures of Gabby's life and came across a little colorful sign created by Gabby, herself, that said this:

IN THE END IT'S GOING TO BE OKAY.
IF IT'S NOT OKAY, IT'S NOT THE END.

I have become friends with Denyse and I see first-hand how she flipped her grief by choosing to serve others. During the holidays she and her other children created their own ministry she refers to as Merry Mailboxes. They placed little gift bags in the mailboxes, around town, of lonely people and those who may need a spiritual lift. It is remarkable and noteworthy of what a difference it makes in a person's grief experience when they choose to serve others and choose gladness over sadness.

Chapter Seven

About Grief

In the beginning, I couldn't talk to anyone. I would not take nor return phone calls. I just plain did not want to cry anymore. Yes, people were worried about me, but I felt that they would have to understand that we all grieve differently. One of the first persons that I reached out to was Norma. Norma is the stepmother of one of Kenzie's besties. I did not know her well and actually met her while sitting at church at Scott's funeral. (Kayla's dad, Scott, lost his life in a motorcycle accident the year prior to Kenzie's death). Scott was like a second dad to Kenzie. I was extremely emotional at Scott's funeral just worrying about Kayla and her sisters and how they would cope. Norma sat next to me and comforted me just by being there. She actually works at a Hospice Home as a grief counselor. So the very morning after Kenzie left us, I called Norma and I asked her for any recommendation that she might have for a grief counselor for Sean and I. She gave me the names of several.

I ended up going to one that was considered Christian based counseling. It did not work out. I remember asking this counselor who was a minister if he would pray with us before we began, and he seemed uncomfortable with the idea and told me that if I wanted to pray that that would be fine. And so I did but, it seemed odd to me that he did not want to take the lead on this. I made my husband come with me to every session and I basically cried for the entire hour. Eventually the counselor requested that I come alone and I declined to go back. Counseling is so intimate, in that one is exposing raw emotion and personal feelings that it really has to be a fit to work. I just did not have this connection with my counselor.

I reluctantly tried attending a group meeting of a well-known organization that supports grieving parents; this at the urging of my friend Pam, who went with me. We visited twice. My sense is that this organization is highly respected and cares deeply for its attendees but, again, just not a good fit for me. The thing that I noticed about the group of people that had attended those two meetings was that most of them seemed to have no hope. Some had been attending the monthly meetings for over twenty or thirty years since they lost their child. They were unable to experience joy, only sorrow, as if their very existence revolved around their child's death. When their child died, they died too.

Norma called me maybe nine months afterwards to invite me to a grief support group that was being held at the Hospice Home. She explained that none of the people in this group had lost a child, but that each had lost a loved one receiving hospice care. She said that she felt that this particular group of people would be a nice fit for me. And it was. There were five other people coming from entirely different circumstances, but none the less, grieving for the loss of their loved one.

Each week was different. I remember one of the first exercises that we were given was to color a heart on a piece of paper. We were invited to color different proportions based on how we were feeling. I recall coloring mine with a large portion black and blue which represented how beat up I was feeling. I remember leaving a center portion uncolored as that was the part that was feeling emptiness. We each spoke to the group and shared a bit about what we had colored and why. At the end of the six week session we were given the same task, to color a blank heart on a piece of paper.

It was amazing to see the transformation that had taken place as Norma returned our original drawings so we could do some comparison. My second drawing included the color green to represent some healing, and mostly red for the immense love I was feeling for my daughter, and even a little purple for joy. What I have come to realize is that a huge part of me died with my daughter; a part of my life that will never again be the same. I have also been awakened to discover more about myself and that I could very well become a better person because of this tragedy. Perhaps this is my destiny, my God given purpose. My daughter's death was purposeful. She has changed so many lives for the better, including mine.

Many books were given to me; spiritual books, books about healing, and books on grief. I have learned that there are several stages to grief and that they don't always come in any particular order. The stages include shock and denial, pain and guilt, anger and bargaining, depression with loneliness and reflection, upward turn, reconstruction, and working through and finally acceptance and hope. I have personally experienced that many things can trigger our grief which is not on the surface. Little things and traumatic events, as well, can stir up deep feelings of loss or hopelessness.

His Inspiration in Stories and Dreams

I found journaling early on to be a wonderful form of self-preservation; and then, started to share on Facebook some of my simple little stories. I received many "likes" and private messages too about how my experiences were speaking to others. I decided to share a few of my stories here. Random stories that may or may not seem to fit in as I retrospectively identify some of the stages of my grief in my writing. I will admit that it is so important to gravitate to what you love. If its art, then paint, draw, create. If its music, then play or sing your heart out. For me, to write is survival. Regardless of how well I may have crafted this small pleasure, it is still the baring of my soul, leaving my thoughts "out there" to be sifted and measured; held or discarded.

Serendipity—May 2013

Today is Mother's Day, my fourth Mother's Day without you. The pain is there but a thin film has managed to cover the gap, with emotion just bubbling underneath. I miss you. I remember the first Mother's Day mere months following your escape into a better place we know as Heaven. I made up my mind (with a big nudge from you) to make the best of the day and booked a white water rafting trip with Sean. It was incredible and I actually found myself saying to your brother "Oh my goodness, this is the best Mother's Day ever"! And then, I looked at him and followed it up with: "Did I just say that"?

Traditionally, you my sweet girl took care of Mother's Day. Once I recall coming back from church to find the house decorated and a wonderful cake that you had baked for me. You were always the life of the party. Our last Mother's Day together you took me out for lunch; my pick of restaurants. You went along with me to my favorite Tai Restaurant (not your first choice). It was wonderful. And the gift that you gave me, now in retrospect so meaningful. A beautiful glass domed desk clock with a heart pendulum. Time, you gave me time.

Since you have left, I have been given the amazing gift of new friends. It is unbelievable how many new friends have been placed in my path for a reason. Now, God is using me to help others make the most of each day moving to the beat of happiness. These new friends have all been given the same unexplainable challenge to create a new life without their child. I have to remind you that I always believed it would never happen to me!

My most recent gift was a new friend that I met on a semi-empty plane from Atlanta during my return trip from Alaska. She plopped down in her seat beside me and announced "I guess this is me"! I smiled and thought to myself what a positive individual, so happy and confident. She proceeded to peruse her calendar on her tablet and I noted that she seemed busy and probably on her way back from a business trip. We exchanged pleasantries and I began to talk to her about Zumba and other common interests. When I eventually got around to talking about you, Kenz, as I always do, she gasped and burst into tears. She said to me: "Do you believe in serendipity"? She grabbed my hand for dear life an explained that she had just lost her daughter three months earlier. She looked into my eyes so intently and asked: "How do you get through the firsts of everything?" We had a very long and heartfelt conversation on that two and half hour flight and exchanged numbers. No mere coincidence that she was placed in the seat next to me on that semi-empty plane.

This Mother's Day my new friend and I will be whitewater rafting at the Zoar Gap. This is becoming a tradition for me. We will challenge our emotions to dare to be anything but happy on this Mother's Day celebrating the lives of our sweet children.

Car Wash ... Car Wash—Mothers' Day weekend 2015

It's the week of the upcoming Mothers' Day and she got my attention once again. Bob and I had been up at the camp opening it up for their "sneak /peek" weekend. It is a time where all seasonal residents can open up their camps and get a jump start on yard work. We had taken a ride early Saturday morning and Bob suggested that we stop for another coffee. He went in while I sat in the car. On the street in front of where we were parked, there were some girls holding signs and yelling, "Car Wash, get your car washed". As I sat there and glanced over, one of the girls got my attention. She was wearing her soft ball team jersey with the number 10 on it. She reminded me of Kenzie as she seemed really spirited. She started a chant, "What do you say when I say CAR"? And the other girls repeated after her. I was thinking this would have been Makenzie leading a chant. Anyway, as I sat there, I could sense Kenzie saying to me: "mom, you need to do it; get your car washed or at least make a donation". I started to think about all of the fundraisers that Makenzie was involved in for soccer or church youth group events, and of how very kind people were to support their endeavors.

When Bob came back with our coffees, I asked him if he had a ten dollar bill and told him that I would like to make a donation. He suggested that we just go over and get my car washed. Now, I need to add here that neither one of us ever get our car washed at these fundraisers for fear of scratches from the gravel that ends up in the wash rags and sponges. For him to suggest that we get my car washed was a bit out of sorts.

So, we drove across the street and around the back of the building and got into line for the car wash. When it was our turn and they started to rinse my car off, a woman who seemed to be one of the moms, stepped up and started snapping pictures of my "KENZ10" license plate. I was surprised and anxious to know why. When I had the opportunity, I jumped out of the car and ran up to her and asked why she had taken pictures of my plate. She apologized by saying, "I'm sorry, I'll delete". I explained that I only wanted to know why. She replied by saying this, "We thought that it was fun. You see, our daughter's name is Makenzie, and we call her Kenz, and her number is 10". Wow! I got teary and told the woman about our Kenzie and she gave me a hug. I gave her my Kenzie bracelet and asked her to give it to her daughter and ask her to wear it for me. She said that she would.

Later that day, I went back by myself to the same group of girls. As I drove down the street they were cheering and pointing to my license plate. I parked the car in that same parking lot and went over to the girl wearing the number 10 shirt and introduced myself. I told her about her mom taking those pictures at the car wash across the street, and asked her if she would let me take a picture of her in her number ten uniform. She obliged, and told me she was sorry for my loss. As always, it is such a great affirmation to receive these little gifts.

When we arrived home the next day, which was Mother's Day, there was another little surprise waiting for me in my mailbox. There was a hand written note with a red heart on the front of it and something attached with a paper clip. It was a note from Clare, my daughter's prior pre-school and kindergarten teacher. This is what her note said:

Dear Marcy,

> *Surprise! This came my way on May 1 as I was sorting materials. I hope it brings a smile.*
> *I know that her birthday was/is in May. I feel if she could write you a postcard from*
> *Heaven, it would be filled with love, joy, and wonder–just like this postcard from*
> *Bermuda. Happy thoughts and blessings coming your way, Love, Clare.*

Clare had attached with a paperclip the very postcard that Makenzie had sent to her from Bermuda, when Kenzie was only five years old. My dad, Kenzie's grandpa had taken us on a cruise to Bermuda. It was so sweetly written in her little five year old handwriting. Receiving this little note and post card in my mailbox was great. It was another blessing and perhaps a reminder that she is watching over me. God's perfect timing to help a mom who was dreading Mothers' Day. Additionally, that same week, I received a message and a picture from my dear friend Betty. Betty and I had met on that very cruise and have been friends all these years. She too, had stumbled onto something unexpected. It was a picture of all of us during our trip to Bermuda. I had told no-one except for Bob about Kenzie's postcard from Bermuda received earlier in the week.

My Daughter's Room
Shelves adorned with life's sweetest treasures,
Soccer trophies, lavender fairy, Rubik's Cube and a jar of glitter.
Stuffed animal pals propped on the satin covering of her bed,
Diary hidden beneath the mattress, Her music player with earbuds left at the head.

Proud painted art work dress the purple walls,
With lights twinkling at ceiling level.

Colorful paper lanterns hang in a corner,
Balancing a butterfly wind chime placed by my daughter.

Backpack and athletic bag just as she left them
Dirty socks, worn cleats, tiny folded notes passed between school friends.
The cork board displays photos, dried prom corsage, and Chinese fortune,
Speaking volumes of her world, now such a blessing.

#10 soccer T draped on the closet door,
Yearbooks tossed randomly on her messy floor.
My daughter's pendant-cross still dangles from the mirror;
As my tear-stained Bible lays waiting on the dresser.
It's been five long years since that fateful day.
I survey her room paralyzed
I cannot change a thing.

Finding the Hidden Treasures—July 2015

*My husband and I got up early with hopes of catching the sunrise. He wanted to try to find treasures at the beach as I had given him a metal detector for his Father's Day gift this year. The sky was glorious this morning, such amazing colors. Like "**Joseph's Technicolor Dream Coat**", I imagined. As I snapped beautiful pictures of the images before me, I instinctively drew a large heart in the sand with Makenzie's initials as I did so often. Immediately, the first person I thought to share my pics with is Kenzie's dad. I knew he would be up as he too is such an early riser. I rarely share anything about Kenzie's dad as it does not seem appropriate. It is a distant chapter in my life, but also a very important one. After all, he with God's blessing, helped create our wonderful children. Through much fun and laughter, as well as significant heartbreak, he shares a lot of my story.*

Her dad has suggested that I have left him and our son out of this journey since losing our daughter/sister, but it is simply not about anyone else. It may appear self-centered, but just trying to recalculate this, my road map, as he and Sean have to do for their own sustenance. My heart aches for them and I would like nothing more than to wave my magic wand and make this misery disappear for them. For me, it might be different. I embrace it; the sadness, the joy, and even excitement, tripping, stumbling, recovering, and now racing through this 100K challenge.

So I sent the sunrise pictures that I snapped this morning, and in return he sent back pics of our beautiful Makenzie. Grief is different for everyone at so many levels. How we survive creates intricate layers of who we are and where we may be headed. I am thankful that God has given us this emotion to help us reconcile and grow.

I am so grateful for Bob, my husband, who, like me, likes to search for treasures in extraordinary ways. Today's catch for him: 16 cents and a man's cuff link. For me, this is another essay to share my journey.

Yes, if you cry out for discernment, and lift up your voice for understanding,
If you seek her as silver, and search for her as for hidden treasures;
Then you will understand the fear of the LORD, and find the knowledge of God.
For the LORD gives wisdom; from His mouth come knowledge and understanding. Proverbs 2:3-6

Baby Makenzie with her dad Benny—

A Song from Above

In the beginning I heard it more often, and now I still occasionally hear it. I believe that it is my Kenzie telling me, "Mom, pay attention to what's next"! The song that she picked is called **Love Story by Taylor Swift.** She knew that I would recognize it anytime I heard it.

When we were searching for Makenzie's first car it was such a challenge. We looked at car after car and nothing seemed to fill the bill with what Kenz wanted and staying in our price range. Of course she wanted something sporty; she was a teenage girl. I wanted something safe, and now in retrospect, realize my girl had me where she wanted me: we settled on sporty. One Sunday when I was driving to church, I saw this beautiful little red sporty grand am, that had, as my son would put it, awesome rims! It had Kenzie written all over it. I stopped and looked but realized it was out of our league. I went past it several other times and eventually called on it. The owner agreed to take it into the Pontiac garage and have it "gone over" at my expense. After we did this, several items were flagged, and thus the price radically was reduced. I decided by having our great mechanic Marty fix it, we could probably get it down to our price. Kenzie hadn't even seen it yet. I called the owner and he agreed to drive it to Makenzie's workplace, the nursing home just up the street. My plan was to show her and possibly take her for a test ride during her break. When she came out of the front door at the nursing home, the look on her face spoke volumes. This was her dream car. We took it for a ride with the owner and decided to buy it.

Kenzie loved her car. She outfitted it in zebra-striped seat covers. She had a little zebra mascot sitting in the back window; this one was white with black stripes. This girl loved zebras since she was a very little girl.

Kenzie came to me one day and said I have decided on a name for my car. She said "Romeo, from that song by Taylor Swift. Mom, listen to the words; it fits perfect".

So, if you get a chance, listen to this song and its lyrics as it fits so well.

You know, I think of this often how the story of Romeo and Juliet ended; they died together. My daughter was in her dream car with her zebra seat covers and zebra mascot when her life ended. Her car, Romeo died there too, with her.

So I hear this song still, at times least expected, but it usually means that I need to pay attention to something. In the beginning, the song would come on the radio when I was really thinking hard and missing her. I heard it again this morning after I had a tearful conversation with God, and I will pay attention.

Kenzie and her sweet
ride "Romeo"

Sea Glass

As I sat and prayed this morning, the notion of sea glass entered my mind. I started to dwell on it and how it compares to our lives. Have you ever found *a piece of sea glass? Perhaps, it's a tiny treasure to be contemplated. Where did it come from and what was its story? An unwanted now broken discarded object from which the original glass which had its purpose, and then somehow survived the turmoil of the ocean. By going through this process, the turmoil of the sea smoothed and refined its rough edges to soften its exterior creating an end result of simple beauty. I think of the colored glass representing my own emotions; red – love but maybe anger, blue for sadness, green for healing, and lavender – joy. I reflect on the turmoil that has been part of my own life at times. How wonderful, my realization, that with my faith in Christ I can have the assurance that He is perfecting His beautiful image in me. God's own exquisite design and purpose, now like sea glass.*

I think of Heaven and its promise. Perhaps an infinite jar of sea glass filled with beauty that can't be measured nor compared to anything in this life. Exquisite pieces of broken glass transformed into such brilliance; God's artistry beyond my imagination.

Thoughts from My Sister, Sherry

"Losing Makenzie was tragic! Going through the experience with my sister has been both terrible and an unprecedented privilege. I have watched my sister transform. I have shared in her profound sadness; the disappointment of a life forever changed and her dashed hopes for the future with her beautiful daughter.

I have also been honored to watch her come out of the ashes of her devastation and rebuild her world with the help of Makenzie's spirit and friends. Marcy has become a woman of much deeper faith, and loving care for those around her. It would be trite to say that losing a child is ever going to lead to good in anyone's life—but she made the choice to live the way that Makenzie would have. With God's great care, Marcy is alive in a way she never was before".

Quilt Patterns

Early this morning, when I was just lying in bed, I thought of the night before. We attended a fundraiser for our youth group at church, raising funds for the high school aged kids to attend CHIC (Covenant High in Christ). I was smiling as I thought about this beautiful quilt that I now have in my possession, as I won the bid in the auction. I realize the absolute skill, devotion, and time represented in this piece. I also now have in my possession from last evening, a wonderful handcrafted journal. It is made of wood with an intricate carved design on its cover and bound in leather. The empty pages are made of parchment that matches the book. It was created by people in Kenya involved in a ministry called Trading Hope. I start to think about the hands that created this beautiful book and only aspire that I can do it justice as I fill its pages. And finally I begin to think more about writing, as I always do; a fleeting thought that starts to manifest in my mind until I have to write as it won't let me go.

I have this other journal that I only use to write down thoughts of Makenzie, since she left us. On its cover it says this: Families are like quilts...lives pieced together...colored with memories past and bound by love.

Isn't this true though about our lives? I think about all of the people who have come into and been significant in my life; that have been a part of my story. Attending the youth group's event last night at church just brought back sweet memories of growing up as a child in the church. I was surrounded by devoted Christian friends who were committed enough to give me their time in my youth to teach me and bless me with a faith that sustains me to this very day. Funny, that at the time that I was little, I couldn't fully understand why it was so important for me to be at Sunday school and youth events learning about Jesus. Little mustard seeds planted in my soul to eventually take root and grow. I think of my Sunday school teachers and youth leaders who are now gone beyond. I feel regret that I never personally thanked them for the role that they played in my life; intricate patterns woven into my life and bound by love. What a gift-, an inheritance that they have prepared me for in Heaven.

I think of my children, Makenzie and Sean, and the seeds that were planted in their lives by similar selfless individuals who shared their time and their faith and their lives. Maybe a month or so after Kenzie left us I came upon the sweetest gift in her Bible. It was a letter that she wrote to herself from Christian camp when she was a teen. Her camp counselor had asked the cabin of girls to jot down a letter to themselves during their week at camp and the counselor mailed it back to them later on the following year. What a great way to remind them of their experience at camp and to bring them back to those thoughts to ponder. Makenzie wrote of her faith in God and the importance of giving back to Him, in her own words. 115%. Wow, what a gift that camp counselor and my daughter gave to me by allowing me to find that letter, which gives me the reassurance that my daughter has inherited the greatest gift of all!

And so, I leave you with this...never question the impact that you may have on a child. The importance of taking time to share what you know is good and right. You are a thread in the pattern of their lives that has the potential to create a beautiful masterpiece. Like a quilt...intricate patterns woven into a life and bound by love.

Kenzie's Letter to Herself

One of the treasures that I value the most, is a letter that I found in Makenzie's Bible early on. While at camp, in 2008, she had written a letter to herself as her other cabin mates, did as well. Her camp counselor mailed it to her in October that following autumn. I consider the timing of this very important as I also was personally baptized at my church in October 2008. I was asked to share my faith testimony in front of the congregation and Makenzie came and listened. I was extremely nervous as I delivered my testimony to the church. Makenzie told me afterwards that there was not a dry eye in the sanctuary, hers included. We share a love for Christ and our Father in heaven and for this I am so very grateful. Our daughter is in Heaven today; this I know! Here is her letter that she wrote to herself from camp:

Kenzie,

We all fall short at the feet of God. You most likely have sinned since you got home from camp, and you're missing it like crazy. Remember to keep in touch with all the amazing people you've met. We all do fall short at living the life God wants us to live, but try to keep the faith. This second, crack open that Bible, and spend some time alone with God. It's really important to spend 5 to 10 minutes a day with him. Try to live your life 115% for Him and don't be ashamed to share His love. Appreciate mom and dad, they love you so much; just as God does, and He will always love and forgive you. His love is unending.

Love you,
Kenzie

A Bike Ride to Acceptance—October 2015

What a gorgeous day to sneak in an afternoon ride on my bicycle. There is so much beauty to take in during these short autumn days. I headed out as always towards New Hampshire as my heart always calls me in that direction. I stopped at the accident site but this time, only momentarily. Usually when I visit, I look for anything remaining even after these long five years; pieces of glass or plastic from her car, anything tangible as a witness to this colossal event. Today was different. I did not oblige the urge to look for reminders but instead heeded the thought that I needed to keep on riding. As I continued down the road, the thought of my bike riding friend Ralph entered my mind.

My first association with my neighbor, Ralph, was a call from him late at night while I still lived in the city. My husband and I had purchased our country lot to build our house and my husband was there on weekends clearing the wood for the site. Ralph woke me from a sound sleep to introduce himself and to explain that my husband had got the tractor stuck in the mud and they were in the process of pulling him out. He had a fun sense of humor and I had a feeling we were going to be great neighbor friends.

After moving into my house and over the course of twenty three years, Ralph has become one of my most endearing friends. Although he is quite a bit older than I, he has the same love for the outdoors and we have shared bike rides, kayaking, four wheeling, and snowmobiling too. Never could I visit Ralph and his wife without being sent home with a gift of maple syrup. I still visualize him making his rounds collecting sap from the maple trees that border our properties. As close neighbors and friends, we have gotten to know the habits of one another. For instance, I know not to ever call him between 7pm and 8pm as he watches Jeopardy. He is a selfless man who never wants to impose on anyone. One late afternoon after he had lost his wife and was living alone, he called me to ask if I could come over when I wasn't too busy. I eventually went over there only to find him on the ground outside his home lying in a pile of leaves. He had lost his footing and fell and had called me from his phone that he carried in his back pocket. He did not want to impose so spared me the details of why I was going over there.

This past year his health has been declining and he had a fall which finally landed him in a bed in the local nursing home. I have considered it a bit difficult to visit this place as this is where my dad lived his final days and where Makenzie worked as well. I have visited Ralph a few times and each time I found him anxiously waiting to go home. Today though was different. When

I rode my bike there to see him, I found him with company and in good spirits. When I asked how his rehab was going, he reported that he has been cleared to go home. He also added that he is not sure he is ready, as he feels he has the best of both worlds. He can go whenever he wants to. He told me that he really misses not having his license though. When I asked him if he had his license and could drive anywhere, where would he go? He did not miss a beat and said "your house." I consider it awesome that he has come to an acceptance of his circumstance. We had a nice visit and I promised to call him at 7pm. This time I would remind the nursing staff to put Jeopardy on for him.

God's Promise at the accident site

As I rode my bike back to my house, past the accident scene, I stopped only to take a picture of the foliage. Like Ralph, it is awesome that I have come to an acceptance of this place. I can now claim the realization that there is nothing remaining, but beauty and hope as I contemplate God's promise.

A Christmas Tree of Life

As I read posts about loss, especially recent loss and about sadness around the holidays, it makes me think of that first Christmas without Kenz. I recall words from a well-meaning friend: "you will just have to find your new normal". At the time, the words stung! I did not want a new normal. I had made up my mind that I was not going to have a Christmas tree. After all, Makenzie was such an intricate part of the tradition of putting the tree up. I am, for the most part, a procrastinator. I have to feel inspired to do things that matter but, Kenz always wanted the tree up immediately following Thanksgiving. I could usually delay this with my own reasoning for a couple of weeks but then she would haul off and pull the decorations out of storage and get everything going. With Christmas music blaring, she would get the tree situated with lights wrapped on it and a few precious handmade ornaments from kindergarten placed strategically front and center (she knew that I would move these sweet little gems to the back to accommodate my own need for synchronicity and perfection). And then she would ditch me! Opened boxes spread all over the living room floor she would find something else to suit her fancy and leave me to finish the job.

133

Anyway, that first Christmas season I was shopping and as I waited in line, a box of purple ornaments summoned me. I actually got out of a very long line at a cash register to retrieve this single box of ornaments and then get to the back of the line to purchase them. So that first December, Kenzie's friends Nicole and Ashley came and helped me decorate the most meaningful and precious Christmas tree. In some sense, I consider it my Tree of Life that first Christmas. I also shared with Nicole and Ashley about Kenzie's gift of life. It was a very long and tearful afternoon as they poured over the pages of the letters of correspondence that I have exchanged with the recipients. I think we used a full box of tissues that day.

Once word got out about my purple decorated Christmas tree, gifts of ornaments came from so many sweet friends. There were purple, zebra, and butterfly ornaments and purple ribbon bows too! I was mesmerized by the white lights shining on each special decoration and would sit for hours in the evening transfixed in my own thoughts and place of serenity. Perhaps only a tree Kenzie's mom could love? That first Christmas I kept that tree up until Valentine's Day when Bob finally coaxed me and then begged me to put it away.

Nicole and Ashley-Christmas Tree decorating 2010

We have celebrated these past five Christmas seasons with this pretty but eclectic Christmas tree. As I started to work on this year's Christmas tree on the day after Thanksgiving (Kenzie inspired), I did not get too far. Only lights strung on the tree; still pondering, what am I waiting for? It just came to me this morning that I will bring out all the old favorites from years gone by and use them this year. Yes, I will take my most precious and cherished handmade ornaments crafted by tiny hands and strategically place them front and center.

Each person's process of experiencing those first holidays without their loved one is unique. A new normal is unimaginable and even seemingly insurmountable for most of us. Be gentle and kind to yourself and allow the gift; the greatest gift of all to embrace you, love on you, and allow your heart to find peace and comfort. Maybe even joy will be discovered in something as unassuming as a box of purple ornaments or the tracing of a small hand.

Chapter Eight

Making My Ripple

Our Little Girl from Kenya

In 2006, we decided to sponsor a child through Compassion International. I had heard of the need through a Christian radio station that I listen to, during child sponsorship week. The names and bios of children who awaited sponsorship were given and I felt drawn to a little five year old from Kenya. I have always had a special affinity for Africa; although I am not certain why. Perhaps it was my exposure and interest that my mother brought to us as a small child. Our mom had a pen pal from South Africa. Her letters and care packages that arrived were intriguing to me. This friend was a bit of an artist and painted scenes from her homeland. My mother and she were pen pals for over 30 years. Thankfully, they had the pleasure of meeting in person prior to my mom's early death due to cancer in 1995.

After thoughtful prayer, and a conversation with Makenzie about child sponsorship, it seemed apparent that God was leading us in that direction. I called and sponsored Naegu R. the little girl from Kenya. Naegu lived in a placed called Maranantha Village, in Kenya.

One of Kenzie's assignments in Civics class was to share about how impacting the world by small acts can make a difference. She chose to bring in pictures and letters that we received from Naegu and information about her life in Kenya. Her presentation was warmly received and I believe that little mustard seeds were planted to harbor thoughts of compassion and the small difference that each of us can make in this world. I knew that the seeds had already been planted in Kenzie's heart.

One of my big dreams now is to travel to Kenya to meet Naegu and learn more about her life and the needs of her immediate family and her community.

A Hot Air Balloon

I headed back to visit my friend Liz, the owner of the little shop in Portsmouth where a couple of years earlier we met. She was the woman who gifted me the beautiful purple Tree of Life pendant, after I found that sweet little note on Makenzie's birthday weekend. "Keep calm, cuz I love you mom".

This subsequent visit, I spent time sharing with Liz about some of the beautiful amazing reminders that I have received, and about this book that I am writing about this incredible journey. I also explained to her about the things that I feel God has placed on my heart, including a possible upcoming trip to Kenya next spring to visit Naegu, our sponsored child.

As I was talking to Liz about my book and my heart felt plan to travel to Kenya, she asked me what I thought the title of my book will be and without hesitation I told her, **"Wish You a Goode Journey"**. This too, was a God wink as my friend Norma puts it, as this title was given to me by Kenzie herself.

After we spoke for a bit, I took a stroll around her quaint little shop, Wanderlust, looking for possibly another note or sign of some sorts from Kenzie...but nothing. So I went back and stood at the counter to finish up our visit. I said to my friend that I was hoping to find something that I just had to have. Then I looked down, and right there at my fingertips on the counter, was this little sign which I knew I had to have. It was a little glass frame, approximately 3 x 5, and on one side of the glass frame there was a hot air balloon constructed out of map material, and across it the word, **JOURNEY**. On the other side of the glass frame was glued a tiny compass, passport, and stamps. Was this a sign that I am going to Kenya?

I have received mixed ideas from friends and family members about this trip to Kenya. There were warnings from some and also heartfelt encouragement from others. But what did God want me to do? I decided to continue to pray for wisdom and discernment.

A few weeks later, I received an email from Compassion International inviting me to volunteer at an upcoming event about child sponsorship. This event was being held in a neighboring town. Although not close to me, I was considering it, as I pondered how little of my personal time I actually give to the Lord for volunteering. A few days went by and then I received a phone call from Kayla, Kenzie's best in the whole wide world friend. Kayla had just moved to this same town. Hmmm, was this a coincidence, or an affirmation that I needed to get involved with this volunteer event? I spoke to Kayla about it and she agreed to volunteer with me and so we did the event.

I continued to pray about God's wisdom and guidance on what to do about going to Kenya. The clock was ticking as I needed to register soon before the spaces filled up. My husband was not excited about the prospect of me going so very far away. There was also the subject of how I would finance such a trip. I did not enjoy these verbal exchanges with my husband as he had valid points on many accounts. As I prayed one morning to God and asked him to give me signs of affirmation about what to do, I received a picture text from Bob out of the blue. It was a field of sunflowers where a hot air balloon had just landed nearby! Oh my goodness, I believe that our Father in heaven adores this little game with me. I know for certain that He wants me to trust Him. My obstacle is that I need desperately to have my husband's blessing on this. It would be so much easier if he wanted to join me on this adventure of a lifetime. Although I am not planning to go to Kenya, in March 2016, I will continue to seek God's wisdom as I try to follow His will.

Pastor Rick

Although I am usually unable to get a signal on my car radio, for the Christian radio station that I like, one morning I tuned in just in time to hear an advertisement of an upcoming Christian Writers Workshop. I immediately took down the number and called to inquire. I spoke with one of the people who would be presenting at the event, Rick Blasdell. Besides being a pastor, Rick is a non-fiction author and he was going to share a bit about his experience writing and publishing his book, **"One Life to Give"**. I was happy that I successfully registered for this event. Writing this book is my biggest Why in life—truly a God given impulse that won't leave me.

As I headed up to Burlington, Vermont which is a two plus hour trip, I sensed that God was speaking to my heart a few times, reminding me to pay attention to the signs. Since I had my directions plugged into my GPS, I knew it was not about navigation to the conference. I noticed the beautiful purple flowers on the highway heading north. Vermont has breath taking scenery, for sure.

At the conference, I had the pleasure of meeting Pastor Rick Blasdell, the person with whom I initially called and registered for the conference. Rick's published book is a compilation of a series of journals that he kept during his mission work traveling to seven different countries over the course of his lifetime. During our break, I purchased a copy of his book and asked him to autograph it. He asked me if there was anything special I might like for him to write and I merely asked him to jot down a scripture as it comes to his heart and mind. This is what he wrote: "Marcy may this book be an inspiration to you right when you have the need".

Blessings,
Rick Blaisdell

Joshua 1:8

Of course, I could not wait to look up Joshua 1:8 to learn what it might have for me.

This is what it says:

This Book of the Law shall not depart from your mouth, but you shall meditate in it day and night, that you may observe to do according to all that is written in it. For then you will make your way prosperous, and then you will have good success.

It was perfect! I had been praying as I write my book that I might be connected with someone who would help me be accountable to my faith. It is so easy to be led astray or to veer away from the path, God's intended path. I believe that God hand-picked Rick, my new Christian friend to help me stay accountable. The fact that Rick had also been to Kenya was another "AHA" moment for me.

During the lunch break, Rick came to our table and asked if he could join us for lunch. As we sat and visited, I told him about this book that I am writing about my journey in losing Makenzie. I also told him that I had sensed God's voice tell me to pay attention to the signs during my drive up that morning. Rick smiled the biggest smile and he pointed to my book that I had just purchased and he had autographed. He told me to read the chapter on his visit to India. He then explained that during his trip there, his first grandchild was born and he was notified via email. His first grandchild was named Mackenzie. Wow!! Another God wink, if you will.

No More Wrinkles/ It's His Plan

I joined a wonderful direct selling company, Nerium International, in November 2012. I do believe that this was His plan. Never in my wildest imagination would I have thought that this would be a part of my journey. But I have certainty that God placed me here for His purpose and to help me. You see, this opportunity that I said yes to, filled a very large void for me, in my life. I have met amazing people and many are now such good friends. God has placed so many good people in this business for His purposes and to help transform their lives. During just the first year and a half, I was introduced to 11 people who had recently lost a child. Some had faith, others completely lost. I would meet them on my own, while sharing my business, and I also received phone calls and emails from other associates in the business, asking me to reach out to someone who had just lost a child. It amazes me how God works to fit broken pieces together.

Selling anti-aging cream, at first, was a bit scary for me. I have learned to enjoy talking with just about anyone and now sharing our incredible story. As I started to really pay attention and ask God to place the right people in my path, there definitely was a pattern. I do believe that God is using me in this business to share my faith and my daughter's story. The company's motto is Make People Better. They challenge us to better ourselves through self- development and challenge us to make our ripple in life by giving back, in whatever capacity that might be. It is all about giving back. (For more information, please visit www.saturdayblessings. org). It amazes me how God fits the pieces together if we just ask and then have faith and allow it to happen. His plan is so much greater than mine! Although I have yet to make my cool million with this endeavor, I believe what I am gaining is far more valuable.

Will you set your eyes on that which is not? For riches
certainly make themselves wings; They fly away like an

eagle toward heaven. Proverbs 23:5New King James Version (NKJV)

Since, my pastor friend, Rick Blaisdell, selected the above verse to fit in here, I asked him to explain this verse and why he selected it.

"In your last sentence, you expressed a great spiritual truth in that you have gained far more than any amount of monies or riches. This verse, for simplicity's sake, is addressing motives and attitude of the heart toward earthly treasures and what some do, or are willing to do to gain them. It reveals the real truth of the danger of putting our trust in something so temporary and uncertain. It is far better to trust in the solid and certain foundation of the steadfast, unsearchable riches of knowing Christ in all aspects of life. In the end, my spirit will fly like an eagle to heaven, but any worldly gains or wealth will not go with me in a separate suitcase". Rick.

I met Julie, one of my dearest friends in this business, early on. We were meeting at another friend's house to create our "WHY" boards. Why boards are, in essence, goal boards that are created to help remind us of why we are involved in this company, and of how we are going to make the world a better place by creating our ripple. As I placed a picture of Naegu, my little sponsored African daughter, on my board, I glanced over and saw Julie pasting pictures of all these little dark faced children. We got to talking and she shared that these were her little "munchkins" from Haiti. Julie supports an orphanage in Port au Prince and has for several (eight +) years. She dreams of helping this orphanage in a much greater way. My dream is to someday go to Africa to meet Naegu, and learn more about her needs and the needs of her family and community. My greatest "why" my "why that makes me cry" is writing this book, to share my faith and honor the memory of my daughter. My greatest why has come to fruition! I believe that this company has facilitated my growth, and I am so grateful.

One of my favorite business blessings happened during a trip to our annual meeting which was held in Long Beach, CA. I decided ahead of time to also plan to see one of my high school "besties", PJ. I planned a visit to her home in Manhattan Beach, CA which is about thirty minutes away. It was so wonderful to be able to stay with her and visit with her family around the conference. PJ invited my girlfriend Kathy and myself to participate in one of her family ministries which she does every Saturday morning. The ministry is called Saturday Blessings and she and her family and a friend from her church go to L.A. and feed the homeless in the wee early morning hours. PJ's daughter Meghan came home from college with a few friends on Friday and spent Friday evening building 96 bagged lunches to be distributed. I truly can't say that I know too many college-aged kids who would spend their Friday evening in this manner, but I have to say that Meghan and her friends seemed pretty remarkable.

We got up at 4 A.M. that morning and drove into L.A. It was still dark, very dark. As we drove along the streets we saw make shift shelters and tents and people sleeping in tattered bedding along the sides of the road. These homeless people knew PJ and her daughter. Some seemed to be expecting them. PJ explained that we could talk to the people if they wanted to talk. If we came upon someone sleeping, we were to just leave the bagged lunch next to them. One man who I gave a lunch to had a cat. I asked him if it was his cat, and he sort of laughed and said he guessed so since it seems to follow him wherever he goes. I had noticed that PJ had packed some cat food and dog food and so I ran to the car and grabbed a can of cat food and brought it back to the man so he could share it with his furry friend. As I passed by one of the other persons who I had given a bag to, I noticed him crouched over a stone wall behind him and I wondered what he was doing. He was brushing his teeth. The bags not only included food but, also toothpaste, a toothbrush, and other toiletries.

Saturday Blessings also provides some clothing. PJ's friend, James, had a trunk full of donated men's clothing and PJ's trunk carried the women's clothing. The people would come up and ask for socks, or boxers, or shoes, or just something warmer to wear. Many of them only spoke Spanish and so Meghan served as their interpreter. Some of these people had a sincere fondness for Meghan. Who wouldn't? She is this sweet red-headed caring young girl who has a vibrant personality. Her compassion was evident. A larger woman came up and asked for some pants. We searched through the things and PJ pulls out these pants. She said to me: "Hey Marce, look!! Zebra pants"!! I couldn't believe it. Zebra something seems to always make its way into my day to serve as a reminder of Makenzie. I asked PJ to take my picture, even in the dark, holding up these zebra pants before we gave them to the woman who needed pants. Afterwards, when we were looking at the pictures that we had taken, this one was amazing! All that could be seen was me holding up the pants from my waist down and this large orb of light surrounding my face. Of course, I instantly felt that she was there with me. Participating in Saturday Blessings was an absolutely incredible and humbling experience. I am truly grateful that I was invited and honored to call PJ one of my besties. She is truly making her ripple and giving back. (www.saturdayblessings.org)

An Estate Sale—June 2015

Bob and I enjoy venturing out on Saturday mornings when we are at the coast. On one Saturday, we headed out but made a stop at the local grocery store as Bob wanted to get something. As I waited outside in his vehicle, I noticed the woman in the car next to me applying make up to her face. Being in this company, I try to share my product/opportunity with two people per day. So right there before me was my first "share" as she seemed a likely candidate for anti-aging cream. She obviously cared about her face applying cosmetics, so I went for it! As I knocked on her window, she was startled but recovered nicely. I took out my phone and asked her if I could share some before and after pics and she graciously agreed. As we visited, she explained to me that she had stayed the night at her daughter's home unplanned and thus unprepared and so she raced out to get some moisturizer for her face. Upon finishing up with this woman, I gave her a business card and asked her to look at my website and offered to share a sample. I then said goodbye and jumped back into Bob's truck and awaited his return.

As we drove up the street, we came upon a business that was having an estate sale, and so we stopped. As I walked into the yard, the owner came to greet me. She shook my hand and I asked her if she was closing her business and she smiled and explained that on the contrary, she had just done some major renovations and invited me upstairs to check it out. Her business offers alternative therapies such as massage, reiki, and hypnosis. When we got upstairs, I was amazed to see this beautiful space decorated in purples, lavenders, and zebra print. Amazed! As she showed me around, the last office which was locked, had a tree of life adorning the office door. Are you kidding me? There was zebra, purple, and the tree of life all in one place! I told the woman a little bit about Kenzie and all the signs and she said that she wanted to introduce me to the woman with the Tree of Life door who was actually manning one of the estate sale tables outside. I decided to wait to explain more of Kenzie's story with both the owner and the woman downstairs. When we got outdoors, I bumped into another woman. It was the woman who I had just met at the grocery store putting on her moisturizer, in her car. We smiled and said hello again. Melody, the owner of the wellness center, asked if we knew each other and I told her that we had met a little bit earlier at the grocery store. The woman was Melody's mother who had stayed the night. Imagine!! No coincidences, this I am sure.

I decided to leave a bottle of my product with Melody to sample. Who knows? Maybe she would consider selling it in her business. She was excited to try it.

A couple of weeks went by and I received a text from Melody. She told me that she loved my product and was thinking about offering it at her center and wanted a price list. We emailed about possible times to reconnect so that I could pick up my sample and also to talk a bit more about my product. I decided to book a massage with Melody. I figured this would assure me time to get to know her and also share additional information.

So I arrived on the day of my massage; and again I have to stress here, the beauty of the room that Melody gives her massages. The walls are painted in a shade of sage green and the linens in the room compliment in shades of lavender. She has a pretty zebra-striped bench in the corner. There are pretty pictures on the walls. One of lavender flowers, another of a deer standing in a meadow next to a big beautiful tree. Melody and I had agreed in an earlier conversation that there would be minimal to no talking during my massage. She felt conviction in the process of allowing me to totally relax and benefit from this therapy.

In retrospect, I am so happy that she upheld this standard. In my past experiences with massage, I have always felt the need to talk as I felt uneasy lying on the table with a stranger working on me. I felt completely at ease and soon was drawn into rest—not sleep, but definite relaxation and rest. As I lay there I sensed Makenzie's presence. I was not dreaming but, thinking so strongly about her. I was remembering an outfit that she wore quite often and I actually heard her voice, not audible but, I truly heard/felt her voice in my heart. I recalled actual snippets from her life, with conversations. She told me that she is here with me and always is; she almost yelled it to me "I am right here next to you"!! At first I thought about dreams and the lack of dreams that I have had of her; I even asked her in my mind why she does not come to me in dreams. She told me again, that it's because she's right here; literally right next to me. She told me to be sure to go to her friends and ask them about their dreams of her and to get them in my book. As I was considering all of this and not wanting to lose this connection with my daughter, I felt the tears falling from the corners of my eyes. I felt such a deep connection to this place and knew that it is a place I will need to revisit.

When my massage was finished, I spoke a bit with Melody. I told her how relaxed I was and about my experience with my daughter. Melody did not miss a beat but whole heartedly agreed, "Oh yes, she was here—in the room—I felt her". She told me that she got chills a few times as she observed me while providing the massage therapy. She said she sensed that I had some emotional connection. We talked about our "chance" meeting and the fact that I met her mother first, in such an unusual way. She agreed that this was a meeting on purpose. Melody has since joined the business with me and I feel blessed to know her.

Recently something truly incredible happened in the course of my Nerium business. I was sharing the product and business opportunity at a local party, a "wrinkle and wine party", for our new business partners, Jessie and Gail, to help them. When I arrived, a woman, Sue, immediately commented that I looked great and just the same! I smiled as I realized that this woman and I had worked so many years earlier together waitressing at a local restaurant. While I was expecting my second baby, Makenzie, she was also expecting her baby Brittany. This was over twenty three years ago. Anyhow after my business presentation, this friend and I visited for a bit. She explained to me that she had only recently learned about my daughter's tragedy and told me how very sorry she was. She had tears brimming in the corners of her eyes. I thanked her. Then, she went on to say, but there is more. She slowly explained to me that after learning about Makenzie's death and its timing, she realized that it was her husband, Brian, who actually came upon Makenzie when she had her accident five years earlier. I was speechless. So many questions came to mind. Sue explained that her husband was concerned about her meeting me for fear of bringing about too much sadness; but said that he was available to talk, should I decide I wanted to learn more. We exchanged phone numbers. After careful consideration, I set up a time to meet a week or so later. I guess I felt that there was a purpose for this connection and that I needed to see it through.

144

The Bread of Life

When I met with Brian and Sue at their home, Brian was very open and said that I could ask him any questions. He then offered to replay the event for me, as to how everything took place as he remembered things. Brian explained that he used to drive a bread truck and usually drove the back roads between Massachusetts and New Hampshire. On that early January morning, he was headed back after picking up bread in New Hampshire and driving on the road where Kenzie had her accident. He commented on what a beautiful clear morning that it was but that it was bitter cold, and only maybe a mere five degrees in temperature. Brian shared that when he rounded the bend in his box truck he came upon an unusual sight. There was a man standing in the middle of the road with his cell phone wearing his pajamas and slippers. As Brian got closer, he saw Makenzie's car and pulled his truck over to the side of the road just adjacent to her car. The stranger in the middle of the road told Brian that he had to leave, something about having kids in the car waiting and he acknowledged that he had called 911.

Brian got out of his truck and went to Kenzie's car and tried first to open her driver's side door. Her door had hit the fire hydrant; actually wrapped around the fire hydrant, and then bounced off from it as there was a huge indentation in her door. He could not get it open. He immediately went around to the passenger side door and struggled with it a bit and finally managed to pry it open. Brian told me that Makenzie's body was lying across the passenger seat and that it appeared her legs were probably broken as they seemed a bit misplaced. Brian got into the car with our daughter and covered her with his coat as he said he feared for hypothermia not knowing how long she had been sitting there. He brushed her hair away from her face as he said it was very cold and the wind was blowing hard through the car. He told me that the radio in her car was on and he turned it off and that he also noticed that her earbuds were in her ears so she probably had them plugged into her stereo and they came detached after the crash.

He said that he had some time to think about things as he sat there with her in the car, and tried to imagine how the accident occurred. He explained that there was a "pristine" mound of snow that had blown into the median of the road from the surrounding cornfields. By using the word pristine, he said that he meant that the snow mound seemed almost perfect and was only touched by her single tire track as it veered off course. It looked like her front driver's side wheel got caught up in the snow and as she attempted to steer back into her lane, she further got caught up into deeper snow and it was as if her car was sucked into the adjacent fire hydrant like a magnet. Brian told me he felt that she did everything right, and nothing wrong; that he felt that she did not panic and steer erratically, but that she steered the car back into her lane, as there was no evidence of swerved tire tracks, just that one that formed an arch. He did not feel that speed was a factor and said he thought that she may have been going about 35 mph and that from the time of when her tires got hung up to the time she had her crash, may not have been more than three to four seconds. He too, thought it was unbelievable that she would connect with that random fire hydrant and not just head out to the surrounding cornfields. He told me that when her car came to a stop, her front end was facing the cornfields with the fire hydrant to her left. It was apparent that she hit her head very hard from impact.

Brian shared that he had some EMT experience in his past and from all appearances, he believes that Makenzie's injuries were instant and that she felt nothing. "It was like Mohammad Ali with a knock out...it was probably just lights out". As Brian sat there with Kenz, he said he had this deep sense of knowing that this was her time. He said that he also sensed that he was exactly where he was meant to be. When he first arrived at the scene, he said that our daughter was breathing normally and her color seemed good but, as time went on, her breathing became labored and irregular and the color of her skin changed for the worse. The police and ambulance did not arrive until approximately thirty minutes later. We are not sure why. I asked Brian if he thought that Makenzie died there at the scene of her accident. He said she was still breathing when the emergency crew arrived and dismissed him.

While we sat there and talked, I sensed what a caring man this Brian had to be. I thanked him for sitting and taking care of our daughter. A few times during our conversation, he got choked up and explained that he has three daughters, one being the exact same age as Makenzie. Brian asked me how I was feeling about our conversation and if it helped me at all. I told him that yes, it had helped and that it did offer me a sense of relief. How I explained it, was that as Kenzie's mom and ultimate caregiver, I always considered the "what ifs... should haves" scenarios that continued

146

to haunt me. Was it that her tires should have been replaced? Why didn't I personally teach her how to drive/react in the snow and on ice? Was it a deer or animal that crossed her path and caused her accident"? The relief that I felt was that this was clearly a very tragic accident. Our daughter did nothing wrong! I felt peace and affirmation to hear Brian tell me that he felt while staying there with her, a deep knowing that this was her time. I do believe that Brian was hand-picked by God to watch over and care for our daughter. I am so grateful.

Through the vehicle of my Nerium business, God has connected me to people and life scenarios that I may never have found on my own. God continues to bless me as I trust Him.

Proverbs 3:5-6. (My Life Verse)
Trust in the LORD with all your heart,
And lean not on your own understanding;
In all your ways acknowledge Him,
And He shall direct your paths.

A Heart of Trust

From a very early age, like me, many of you were raised in the church. Seeds were planted in our tiny hearts and souls as small children, to penetrate our lives, grow, sprout and eventually burst through to create in us God's reason for our being. Perhaps like me, you have not always trusted.

When things are seemingly going very right in my life it is easy to trust myself by placing first, my own thoughts and ideas. And, sometimes when bad things happen, it is easy to question our faith wondering why God allows bad things to happen, or question where He was in the midst of it.

When Makenzie died, I never blamed God. Admittedly, I was searching for the answers to why such a mysterious accident could happen on that January morning, as she headed off to school. I have never been given all of the answers.

But those seeds of faith that were planted and growing, sprouted and burst through to rescue me by allowing me to see the blessings beyond my despair. What a gift those seeds have been in my life. My walk with Jesus has never been better.

In my meeting of others who have experienced tragedy or hardship in their lives, I see a pattern. For those who are TRUSTING God in the midst of their circumstance, beauty is unfolding for them, as they use the lesson to bring glory to God, who has placed ALL of us here for His intentions; His good purpose.

If you have wandered away from TRUST in God and what His perfect plan is, I encourage you to get back to watering and nurturing those seeds of faith. They are not gone but, merely withered. Beauty will unfold as you marvel at the intricate blessings He is aligning for you. Our God delights as our tiny hearts receive all that is meant for us and more.

I saw this quote by Angela Miller:

> *"The truth is, that hole in your heart, shaped exactly the size and shape of your child,*
>
> *WILL NEVER GO AWAY.*
>
> *But the love that oozes from it has more power to change the world than anything I've ever known".*

Dreams

I believe that God sometimes will use dreams to get our attention. In the Bible, especially the Old Testament, there are many stories of how God used dreams to communicate.

My first dream that I remember came a couple of weeks after she left us. I remember sensing her presence standing next to me, at my bedside. I have a tall four poster rice bed that is high off the floor and she was eye level to me as I slept. Makenzie came to me as a little girl...she said in her little girl voice to me: "thank you mama, thank you mama". I thought to myself as I was sleeping...what is she thanking me for? Then a few moments later, I heard her 17 year old voice say to me in a convincing tone, "You need to check on Kayla". I said to her from my voice in my head: "Why? Is Kayla in trouble?" Her response was only "yes." And then she disappeared. The next afternoon, as I remembered my dream I decided to pick up the phone and call Kayla. I could tell by her voice that she had been crying. Later on I phoned Pam, Kayla's step mom and told her about my dream and inquired about Kayla. Pam indicated that Kayla was having a very hard time. I see my dream as God's way of getting my attention and it worked.

In the beginning, aside from that first dream, I felt panicked not knowing if my daughter was o.k. I needed to hear from her or feel from her the assurance that she is in a better place. I longed for dreams but, they did not come to me. I have recollection of only one or two more times that Makenzie came to me in my dreams. Both dreams involved bright, amazingly bright colors and glorious music. I remember seeing these bright geometrical shapes as my mind traveled through the dream and then I saw my daughter smiling her biggest happiest smile. This is the assurance that I longed for. It was brief but powerful. I thank God for this memory of my dreams. Several of her friends would make a comment on Facebook thanking her for being in their dreams. I would immediately private message that person and ask them to share their dreams. Here are a few:

Adria (Adria climbed Mt. Kilimanjaro in Africa, following graduation. She started a project at school called the Sock Project where 300 pairs of wool socks were gathered and she decided to take them to Africa to the porters as a gift).

On the night before I summited Kilimanjaro, I was secretly doubting myself; my physical ability to continue the climb. We were expected to wake up at midnight to start our climb to the top. Previous hours had me fighting with myself to fall asleep. I had to remember to have my Makenzie Goode T-shirt ready to show off at the summit. That was my priority. So I fell asleep with it next to me anxiously. In

Adria atop Mt. Kilimanjaro with the travelling t-shirt

my dream, I unexpectedly was experiencing Kenzie dancing wildly in a white room with a couple of our other friends. I remember feeling really confused about the scenario because I knew it couldn't possibly be real. But I wanted so badly to be a part of it. Kenzie was beautiful and happily dancing to no music. I remember feeling less and less anxious as the dream went on. Makenzie's smile has always inspired me. And this time she looked directly at me, and without a word, I knew she was laughing at me that I even had a slight doubt in myself. I woke up at midnight, pitch black and freezing, feeling so whole and inspired. Makenzie had reignited my energy and self –belief, as I believe she does for most people who have had her in their lives. I thank her every day for that experience.

Chelsey:

Kenzie was definitely a gift from God. I actually had a dream about her the other day. It was us, all of us girls back in high school together in class. We were talking about Kenz and how we wished so bad that we could see her again, and then all of a sudden, a bright light was outside and we looked and Kenzie was walking and waving and laughing at us. She was wearing some crazy outfit; ha ha, and when we all ran outside to talk to her she ran into the field and kind of disappeared into the light. But, it was a really nice dream and I'm glad I still remember it so vividly. It's funny because I never remember other dreams but I always seem to recall every detail of the dreams that I have about Kenz. I just figured that I would share with you.

Pam

After Kenzie passed, my sweet friend Pam told me about a dream and distinct vision that she had experienced. First the vision, which occurred on the day and at possibly the very moment Makenzie left her body to meet Jesus. It was around 1:00 pm or so on January 30th that Pam saw a vision of Kenzie sitting upright in her hospital bed smiling her biggest smile ever.

Later on, Pam told me of a dream that took her to the site of Kenzie's accident and she saw a river flowing next to the accident. Makenzie was standing in the river, moving away with the current of the water. She was again smiling her biggest smile and waving to Pam.

When you pass through the waters, I will be with you; and through the rivers, they shall not overflow you.

When you walk through the fire, you shall not be burned, nor shall the flame scorch you. Isaiah 43:2

I feel a sense of relief as these things are shared with me. I have never had anyone share anything but pleasure when they dream of her. More affirmations that she is fine and has found complete happiness. I believe that my daughter is with me always. All I have to do is tune her in, so to speak. I can hear her voice resonate in my soul. Deep within my soul, she is still and always will be a part of me. I thank God for this amazing gift of being able to hold on to her in this capacity.

Makenzie's boyfriend Matt told me about a dream that he had experienced shortly after her death. He said that in the dream he was with her at the elementary school in the local town. She was telling him not to worry but that she was happy. He had asked her in the dream if she had experienced pain in the accident, and she told him, "No, not at all".

Matt told me one of his happiest memories was on their first date when they had gone to the elementary school at night-time. It was a warm summer night and they lay on a blanket on the grass and just looked up at the stars and talked.

Matt and Kenzie

Kayla's Dream—(2015)

I've had a lot of dreams over the years where I see and feel as if Kenz is still right there with me, growing and experiencing the same things that I am. (I had one around the time of college for example that we were both driving off together).

My most recent dream is the one that really made me feel like she was still with me and has been during my early pregnancy. The timing of this dream was when I was deciding to tell people of my pregnancy. I had waited those first few months, and a few days before I had this dream, I was thinking about telling you (Marcy). I had the dream and it felt like it was the right week to tell you. I dreamt that we were driving somewhere together, Kenz and I, and we pulled over at a gas station to get snacks. I wasn't obviously showing but I had of course told her that I was pregnant and had cravings. She was running around the gas station store picking out craving snacks for me and she ended up with some different trail mixes. She was picking out the snacks with her contagious energy and smile, just making everything more fun. We went over to the slushie machine just like we used to when we were younger, and I wasn't sure if one of them would upset my stomach, so she poured some of each slushie flavor into cups so I could try them each first. I ended up choosing watermelon, and the rest of the dream was just kind of us going to check out of the store and laughing.

Chapter Nine

Ava's Letter to GG

So, I was hoping to end our story with a WOW....not a wink, but a WOW...and God provided!
Here it is!

Ava's Letter to GG

Nothing is by mere coincidence, I do believe that and at this point believe that most everything has a purpose and I tend to accept the unexpected. Since Makenzie's death I have been introduced to, as well as reconnected to, people for a significant reason. More recently, when I was on social media, a name from my past came up as a "suggested friend". I smiled the biggest smile and immediately sent a friend request to this person. This person happens to hold fun memories for me from back in high school and it makes me laugh to remember the crazy things that we all did. Anyway, so much time had transpired that I was curious what he made of his life. Back then, we led different lives and had a different circle of friends, so we lost touch after graduation. I went off to college in another state, and I learned that he had remained in town and eventually married his high school sweetie, and had a family. As I started to look at some of the posts on his Facebook page, I read the recent condolences extended to him and his family. I put two and two together to realize that he had just lost his mom. I use to see his mom on occasion, as she was a greeter at a local store in town. We would exchange pleasantries and I genuinely liked her. As I read the posts I saw an amazing picture posted, that took my breath away, and I needed to know more.

We exchanged several messages back and forth, as I wanted to share with him about losing my daughter and her incredible story. He asked me if I had seen his amazing picture, and he told me the story that went with it. His grandchildren called his mother GG and I thought it fun to share the same name that my grandson calls me. I am GG (for grandma Goode—I am the Goode grandma! ha ha). My friend, Terry, explained that his eight year old granddaughter, Ava, had written a sweet farewell letter to her GG that she read at his mother's funeral. In the letter, Ava requested that her GG send her a sign to let her know that she made it to heaven and was in the presence of all the other angels. Here is her letter.

Dear GG,

> *I always felt like it was special to have you as a great grand-mother, and now that you're happy in heaven, we are happy because you don't have to suffer to breathe. You are probably here listening to this. As your angel, I should not think of you as gone. We should think of you still with us but we just can't hear your voice, because friends come and go but family is forever. But now you're a guardian angel and you won't be with us on earth as a person, you will be with us in our hearts. I just have one question: Is it true that you are with all the angels? You were always a very important member of our family. I hope you answer this note at the funeral and remember what I said:*
>
> *Friends come and go but FAMILY IS FOREVER....Love, Ava (baby angel Ava)*

At the graveside service following the funeral, Ava placed the letter under some red flowers on her GG's casket. My friend Terry took several pictures there, but didn't experience or see anything extraordinary at that time. They even tried to explain to Ava that her GG may not show her something truly obvious but, that they were certain that she was in Heaven. Later on when they were home and Terry pulled out his phone to look at the pictures that he took, he was filled with wonder. An amazing beam of light shone from the heavens down to that very special place where Ava placed her letter. GG made it!! She was in the presence of our Lord and the angels! As Terry said to me..."Marcy, this is God"!!

Like I mentioned earlier, nothing is by mere coincidence. To see my friend's name flash by on Facebook to give me the thought to reconnect with him, only a few days after his mother passed, is extraordinary. I have to wonder if Makenzie and his mom have met and perhaps had something to do with our getting reacquainted. It was nice and I continue to feel inspired by all of these "coincidences"; or rather God winks.

In loving memory of Marilyn J. Parker from "Baby Angel" Ava and God

I wanted to end this, our story, with hope; this is why I decided to use the above image.

Therefore, if anyone is in Christ, he is a new creation; old things have passed away; behold, all things have become new. 2 Corinthians 5:17

Jesus said to him, "I am the way, the truth, and the life. No one comes to the Father except through Me. John 14:6

These years following Makenzie's death have been filled with sadness, joy, and growth. I have learned a lot about myself and more about how I have come to depend on Christ to lead the way in my life. No one expects tragedy in their lives, nor welcomes it when it happens, but I can honestly say that those that I have encountered who are walking in faith, experience a peace filled transition that provides new meaning to their lives. Hope is secured in the ultimate promise that will be ours in heaven.

This book was written in loving memory of my daughter, Makenzie Mia Goode.

Thanks to God for our amazing girl. I have found joy in the journey. It has been a GOODE journey.

Closing Thoughts:

After Makenzie attended CHIC "Covenant High in Christ" in July 2009 I asked her if any of the break-out sessions or workshops stood out and left an impression on her. She commented on a seminar that she attended about child sexual slavery and how devastating this information was to her. She had also commented to Kayla that she would like to get involved somehow after she graduated from college to make a difference for these young girls; perhaps even somehow incorporating her love of the game of soccer.

Life is Goode

A portion of the proceeds from the sales of our book will be donated to **"As Our Own"**, an organization which rescues girls from sexual enslavement and raises them as their own daughters. We are proud to say that our daughter Makenzie is still making her ripple. For more information: www.asourown.org

Epilogue

Overtime, many of Kenzie's friends expressed their feelings through comments on her Facebook pages. This was a great place to be able to share feelings and for many to realize they were not alone in how they were dealing with this immense loss. I would like to share some of them with you, along with some of their funniest memories. There is a close bond among these friends as they experienced loss, immense loss, so early in life. I cherish each and every one of them and attribute much of my healing to their unequivocal devotion to my daughter's memory.

Memories of Makenzie from Her Besties

Chelsey M.

There are so many hilarious memories that consume my mind whenever I think of Kenzie (which is at least once a day). She had this way of creating a lasting impression on everyone she met, making them laugh so hard they could barely breathe. She was a one of a kind spirit, illuminating pure joy wherever she went and touching the hearts of many, myself included. I can honestly say I have never met a single person who matched Kenzie's spirit and genuine love of life and I am honored to have been a part of her world and I will cherish our friendship forever.

One of the best memories I have with Kenzie is the summer going into our senior year of High School. A group of our friends got together to do a scavenger hunt, where we would get into teams and go around town solving clues in hopes of being the first team to finish. My team consisted of myself, Kenzie, Nicole, Casey, Fran, and DJ and it was one of the best days I've ever had! Instead of focusing on getting the clues, we all found ourselves in the backseat of the car taking hundreds of pictures, Kenzie was such a beautiful girl but if you ever went against her in a "who could make the ugliest face" contest – she would win every time and everyone knew it. I don't think I ever laughed as hard as I did in that back seat. We took so many pictures; it was just so funny! During that night we did all sorts of crazy things, pool hopping, buying .50 cents worth of gas, going to Big Y and taking a picture with an employee wearing an octopus shirt. At the end of the night we stopped at Nicole's house and Kenzie found this weird net thing (I think it was a net that's supposed to go around a dish washing sponge) Anyway, instead of throwing it out she put it in her hair and starting walking around the house pretending she was a hair model. She would walk and strike a pose with this weird net thing hanging out of her hair and she was dead serious about it! It was so funny – Kenzie was known as the girl who would "strike a pose" at any moment with her famous hair flip she always did. We probably took about 200 pictures that day (Kenzie was known as the camera queen) and every now and then I find myself going through that photo album and laughing, reliving that wonderful day we had with Kenz.

Kaylee J.

A time that I felt very connected with someone was actually a very sad time in my life. My senior year of high school, my best friend Makenzie Goode got in a car accident and died. This was the hardest time in my life. Kenzie's best friends and I began to frequently visit her mother, Marcy, and share our feelings and stories of fun times with Kenzie. I received a great sense of peace and relief, being able to have such a great group of friends that we all could talk and vent to one other. This made my group of girlfriends closer than ever and I feel that we all share an unbreakable bond forever. Makenzie brought us all closer together and I feel so closely connected to all my friends back home. This is something that will live with us forever and we will always cherish this genuine connection with one another. We all miss Makenzie terribly and there is not a day that I do not think about her. But I have a great sense of liberation knowing that I will forever share with and bond with an amazing circle of friends as well as another amazing mother figure in my life.

Kenzie's sense of humor and quirky ways always put a smile on my face. Her contagious laughter and fun-loving spirit is what I truly miss the most. Kenzie taught me to be comfortable in my own skin, live life each day to its fullest, and never let the opinions of others get you down.

On our last day in English class together, we were taking a test. Kenzie sat behind me and always loved to be goofy and make me laugh because:
1.   I have the loudest laugh out of our group of friends
2.   She knew the teacher would tell ME to stop goofing off

So, here we are taking our test and the room is completely silent. Makenzie decides to take her UGG boot off (which I know from experience is her smelliest pair of shoes). She put her foot right by my head and just left it there without me noticing. Everyone started to laugh and giggle as Kenzie wiggled her toes to see if I would notice. I sat there wondering what was so smelly, yet trying to pay attention to my test. I turned to my right, and there was Kenzie's bare foot, RIGHT in my face! She was twirling her toes in my hair and everyone was cracking up! I immediately started hysterically laughing (of course being the loudest, I got in trouble) and Kenzie quietly slipped her shoe back on and acted like nothing happened. After class, we laughed and laughed and I couldn't wait to get home and wash my hair... Oh, Kenz.

I always looked up to Kenzie and admired her for her free spirit and carefree ways. I wonder what stories we would be laughing at today and what songs we would be singing at the top of our lungs. Makenzie is truly missed and she will always have a place in my heart. My life has been so positively impacted from her sweet soul and I wouldn't be the person I am today without her.

I love you Kenzie

Kayla S.

We all know that Makenzie was one funny girl, all around goofy and fun loving. I was blessed enough to call her my best friend for 13 years, which means that I have over 13 years of funny memories and laughter that we shared. So, how to narrow it down to one?

Ever since we were little I remember going on trips with each other's family. We would often go to the beach for swimming. One summer day we were with my family at the beach. Off we went into the water, wading out into the waves and jumping around. We were already laughing and splashing and just having fun. My older sister was out with us and we were pretty much the only ones out in that section of the water. So of course Kenz decides to up the laughter, and with every wave that she jumps into, she pulled her swim bottoms down to moon us. We were laughing like crazy; she would jump higher and her pale butt would moon us right as the wave crashed. Then she goes even further, and we look over and she has the bottoms of her swim suit in her hand. She is swinging them around her head and jumping in the waves, and we are just laughing at how crazy she is. That is when we see the kid wearing goggles start swimming our way. Kenz did not expect this so she starts screaming a little and saying "Goggles!" So we are all laughing even harder now as she tries to put her bottoms back on, and then she starts freaking out more saying she dropped her bottoms in the water. At this

Kayla with Makenzie-Besties

point we are all laughing so hard we were tearing up. She was frantic and we were all laughing and yelling goggles, the kid is getting closer and closer, and finally she gets her bottoms back on and we all laugh even harder funnier. I'll always cherish those wild things she did and those that she talked us into doing with her.

Sasha S.

Makenzie brought so much happiness to my life. She still does, and every time I think of her, and every time I think of the many years my family was blessed enough to have her lighting up our lives. She was a source of laughter for my father, even when his lungs were weak with sickness and stress, and she was a friend like no other to my little sister from the moment they met in kindergarten, through the long years of elementary, middle, and high school. Makenzie and Kayla, a pair to be reckoned with, and I still remember their elementary school years of matching outfits nearly as vividly as I remember the matching mischief that never stopped twinkling in their eyes. Then, the two of them, unlike your typical teens and ahead of their time, were totally unafraid to let their weird side shine. They were two beautiful girls making face contortions so grotesque that I couldn't help but laugh at them from the other side of the camera as I smiled through a stitch in my side and tears in my eyes. They were two vibrant lives, laughing through life together, as if it was nothing but a play, and the world was their stage.

I remember standing in my kitchen one day and watching Makenzie literally fly across what I could see of the living room. Kayla was holding the camera and filming Makenzie landing safely on this huge, purple bean bag that was about a foot or two from where Kayla was positioned, the brave videographer, standing her ground. They were always dressing up, creating stories and scenarios (sometimes very elaborate), that they would act out in their films. They were making shots of each other flying through the living room and crazy things of that sort. I still crack up over the stunts, voices, costumes, and disguises they'd put on. Once, after driving a long time to get back home, I walked into my father's apartment to find suspicious darkness—an unfamiliar silence of sorts. I knew that Kayla, Kenzie, and my about nine-year-old baby sister, Yona, were all supposed to be home. I knew they were up to something. I froze. Suddenly, the lights came on. So did a computer placed atop a chair that stood right in my way. Someone pressed play and a video came on. It was the "I Wanna Go to Friendly's" commercial. The girls jumped out and all began singing. As they sang, I realized that the kitchen was decorated with handmade posters that reaffirmed they were creatively trying to tell me, that they really wanted to go to Friendly's. As Kayla puts it now, "Well, you were the big sister and you had a car—and we really wanted to go to Friendly's". They had definitely put a lot of time into this (because, as we know, they really wanted to go to Friendly's). And as they later confessed, they had put Yona to work making posters for their scheme.

The two of them had their own rules and didn't care if anyone else followed them. Brilliant at improv, they made it up along the way. That was Kenzie—living every moment, every second, every hour, and every day. These little sisters of mine, this impossible pair of twin-like minds, taught me by example, how to walk about life untouched by the pressures pressing me to be anything other than myself. They delighted in life, but knew not to take it too seriously (for, after all, they already knew that life could be whatever they made it). It was infectious; infectious like Kenzie's laughter. And the dance parties she never stopped starting. And the way she loved to brighten up your day, to put a smile on your face if she could. Makenzie, to me, is a million goofy faces, laughter that echoes, the tiny five-year-old partner in crime to my little sister, another sister, the beautiful young woman she grew to be, the way she stood her ground and never stopped living according to what she believed. She demanded from life, every second that she lived. I will always remember her in all of these ways, in all these millions of memories. I will always remember the happiness she brought into our lives—the happiness that she still brings to life when laughing and living as a memory in the back of my mind.

Ashley B.

This past year on Kenzie's birthday while reminiscing with one of our friends, one of my favorite memories with Kenzie was shared—"the time we borrowed the shopping cart". Casey, Kenzie and I were cruising around in my car one day after school when we were making a trip to Turner's Falls. Walking down the street we saw an empty, untaken shopping cart. So what would three 17 year old girls do? Obviously try to fit it in a tiny Corolla! We managed this in about 40 minutes. So, there we were cruising around in my car, Kenzie in the back with the shopping cart. We pulled up to our friends auto shop laughing and asking him if he could paint it pink and put a system in it for us. We got back to my street and sneaky as we could took the shopping cart out of the back seat. Kenzie jumped in the shopping cart and Casey sat on the hood of my car holding the handle to the

BFFs with the infamous shopping cart

cart. There we were inching down the street to my house with me in my car, Casey on the hood of my car and Kenzie in the shopping cart video-taping us being crazy. There was never a time when Kenzie was around that someone didn't have a smile on their face or wasn't laughing hysterically.

DJ M.

There is no question in my mind that Kenzie was by far the craziest friend I have ever had. She always did whatever she possibly could to keep a smile on your face and to cheer you up when you were feeling down. I would have to say that my greatest memory of her would be one day when she came over to my house. I am honestly not even sure how all of this started but this is the greatest memory I have of Kenzie. We decided to get dressed up in these old dance costumes I had that were covered in fringe. We also wore black tights, underwear over the tights so it could be seen under the dress, these ugly hand knitted shawls, old sneakers, and my old cheerleading medals around our necks. I decided to wear a Disney princess crown while Kenzie wore a headband across her head like a ninja.

We went out into the woods behind my house and just spent hours taking crazy pictures of each other. I always loved taking silly pictures with my friends but Kenzie always knew how to take it to the next level. I will always have that memory stored away in my mind and I always bring it back when I need a laugh. I am lucky that I was best friends with such a silly soul and I am even luckier that I get to keep that part of her with me always.

Alyssa S.

Kenz had a quality that not many people possess, she brought laughter and happiness to everyone she encountered. Every memory I have of her is full of smiles, the way life should be. It never mattered what I was doing with Kenzie, whether it was playing soccer, going to nature's classroom, sitting through a boring class, taking a long ride on the bus, hanging out with friends at the lunch table, or having sleepovers, she always made the experience entertaining and fun! I will never forget the time Kenzie came to my house for our first sleepover together. I had worried all day about what we were going to do during the sleepover and whether or not our friends were going to have a good time. Kenzie was the first to show up and instantly I knew it was going to be a great night. She made all of my worries disappear. There wasn't much to do on the rainy night of the sleepover, so we decided to watch a scary movie. Half way through the movie, Kenzie grabbed the remote and placed the movie on pause, at the perfect second where the "scary" character was making a repulsive face. Kenzie had all of us get up next to the paused screen and pose with the character (Kenzie named him Clyde). For hours we did a photoshoot with Clyde until our camera memories were full. I can honestly say that I have never laughed so hard in my life as I did that night; we laughed until we cried. Who would have thought that something so simple and so silly could stay with us as a memory for years of our lives? Kenzie's memory is a constant reminder to me every day that life is not about worrying about things that might go wrong in our lives, but rather about spending the time we have making memories, being happy, taking chances, and remembering that Life is Goode".

Casey D.

Kenzie and I did driving school together. We developed so many memories from pictures, songs, places we drove, sitting in class, to even driving stories with Bob, the driving instructor. We'd run his errands for him and never had a better time than driving around town, laughing with him.

Alyssa H.

I had played soccer with Kenzie since middle school, and we both got to be captains together (along with Franimal too). Kenz was tough on the field, a leader, and one of the most fun people I ever knew. At practice you could find her working hard on her skills, or running around mooning people. Needless to say, she was goofy and wild. She was generous too; in fact, she helped me get one of my first jobs working with her at the nursing home. Even though it was work, and it wasn't the cleanest or most fun work, we had fun working together; and man do we have some stories. On our breaks, soon after Kenz got her license, we would just go sit in her car and talk and listen to music. One day, we got pretty bored just sitting there and decided to go for a ride. As a new driver, Kenz wasn't supposed to be driving with anyone under the age of 18, in the car, so naturally, we felt like rebels. We drove to her house to get popsicles (we were definitely rebellious, I know). But then, on our way back from our little joy ride we passed her mom, Marcy, on the road. Remember, Kenz had just got her license and wasn't supposed to be driving anyone. Kenzie panicked, and sped away and pulled in behind a building to hide. We both ducked just hoping that Marcy hadn't seen us. Less than a minute later though, in pulls Marcy pretty upset (Romeo was pretty hard to miss, being bright red and all). Marcy instructed me to get into her car and I had to ride back to work with Marcy and Kenzie's grandpa. We both worried later on, thinking about every possible awful thing that could happen; she could lose her license, or even her car! Everything worked out okay, but we learned not to mess with Marcy (he he! Love you Marcy!)

Some Facebook Posts

Katie E.
Reading all of these wall posts makes me cry sometimes because you're such a meaningful person—so many people care about you and most of all love you to death. I just had to share with you. I've been seeing this one butterfly over and over again. It looks like the same one each time; it reminds me of you.

Stephanie T.
Everyone knows you're still around. When it was raining and everyone got sad this weekend, I was still thinking on the bright side that the sun would come out, and then I looked up in the sky and I saw a butterfly fly by. All I could do was laugh and some people looked at me like I was crazy but the next thing you know the rain stopped, and it began to be sunny out. Thank you for making that impact on me to always think positive and be happy and believe and hope that anything is possible. Just like the rain turning into sunshine. Thanks for always being right there with me.

Joey L.
Rest in Peace, Kenzie Goode. Thank you for always looking over me. I know you're up there watching over all of us, keeping us safe. There isn't a day I wish I couldn't take that day back. May you shine upon me and guide me on my way. Rest in Peace. As you danced in the light with joy, love lifted you; as you brushed against this world gently you lifted us.

Meghan H.
Funny how after all this time, there are still days here and there that feel like January 30th. Days where it is so hard to accept reality, and with moments where it seems impossible to crack a smile, even with all the optimism in me. I really miss you. Always so nice to come here and see all the people that continue to keep you in their thoughts. It really is beautiful.

Tirena R.
It's been too long Kenzie. I think of you and miss you every day. Keep shining down on us.

Cody R.

Forever in our hearts will be Kenzie Goode, she was a daughter to loving parents and a friend to everyone who knew her. Through the years we were blessed to have her with us, she showed how compassionate and loving a human being can truly be. And now she brightens our life from above. Every sunny day we know Kenzie is smiling down on us, and every rainy day something might have gone wrong up there but we can still see her smiles when these couple of rays of sunshine peer through the clouds. We will never forget her and she will always in in our hearts. Some day we will be with her and be able to see that beautiful smile that she is so famous for. MMG, forever in our hearts.

Leah G.

There is this bridge, near my school. The first time I drove over it, I remember the sunset was beautiful. I said "I feel like I am driving up into heaven"! Just about a month ago, I noticed a zebra as graffiti on the cement wall that splits the two directions of traffic. I always drive by waiting to see it, almost feel like I'm saying hi to you. The other day I noticed another zebra was added, facing the other zebra and in between them both is a monarch butterfly. I thought I was seeing things, but I think it's just you.

Aubriana R.

Last week when I was giving blood, "Don't Stop Believing" came on. I love when you send me little signs that you're still with me.

Andrew S.

I've been staring at the screen for the past 20 minutes trying to think of something to say to you; then I realized, I already talk to you every day and it's knowing that you're listening that makes me keep going. Thanks for helping me now and in the past, I miss you so much. Drewsie baby

Nick D.

It was great to see your mom today. I don't really know how to feel when I'm in your house, but I definitely feel you there. Just the smell reminds me of you. I went right to your bench at Pioneer after I left so I could see it for the first time. It's perfect. We all want to know the answer of where you are and what you're doing, but that's an impossible concept to grasp. Sometimes I find myself reaching for things to connect you to, or just waiting for something to happen. But maybe all the signs that I need from you are right there in front of me. If I know that you are always with me, why do I need something spectacular to happen? Life itself is spectacular enough because it is over at the moment we least expect it. The answer to all our questions will be revealed in time, but for now I will accept anything that gives me comfort; and there are a lot of things. You continue to affect people here on earth long after you have gone. I have struggled lately with the thoughts of life after death; maybe because I just don't want to have to face the fact that there are things we will never understand or know. But I have to believe that your spirit lives on, doing the things that make you who you are and helping others along the way. You can't assure us of anything, so we just have to trust that we will see you again. Love you Kenzie.

Nicole D.

Every day you amaze me. I love you.

Matt L.

Matt, who was Kenzie's boyfriend, was quiet. He has not relayed much in regard to his sadness, but has tried to stay upbeat and positive. The one thing I remember in the weeks following was something that his mom shared with me. Matt played baseball for his college baseball team as a pitcher. Every game that Matt pitched in, he would draw Kenzie's initials in the sand on the baseball mound before he pitched a game. He was a good and devoted friend and my daughter loved him.

February 28, 2016

Corinne N.

Hi Marcy. My name is Corinne and I went to camp with Kenzie many years. I'm not sure if I ever told you my story, but after seeing how you have taken all that she has done and written a book about it, I don't want you to miss any pieces that may greater influence you and show you the good that Kenzie has done even after her passing. Three years ago on Sunday, February 24, 2013, I was on my way back from CT to NH where I was going to school. As I passed over the New Hampshire border, it had just started to snow. At that time, I was not as careful of a driver as I should've been, and

I lost control of my car. I spun off the road, on the opposite side, driving backwards into a small wooded area. I do not remember what happened before or during, but what I do remember is waking up. I woke up whimpering, in pain, and noticed there was a girl sitting next to me, holding my hand, telling me the ambulance was on its way and everything was going to be okay. I got to the hospital and unfortunately didn't catch the girl's name. I had suffered a concussion, three broken ribs and had to get seven staples in my head. If my car had been just a few inches further into the woods, my head would have smashed into a tree and I probably wouldn't be here today. The next morning, I got a message on Facebook from a girl I did not know; she was the one who sat with me in my car the previous night. Her name was Bryanna N. and we had one friend in common Kenzie. The two of them went to high school together. I burst out in tears knowing very well that Kenzie had sent her to watch over me that night. I feel extremely blessed that Kenzie had been my guardian angel that night and I'm sure she continues to be. Once I saw the book you will be publishing, and read the back, I yet again got chills and started crying. In my old car, the car I was driving that night, the car that I totaled, where Bryanna was on my passenger side holding my hand, was a Chinese fortune taped to my rear view window... "Wish you a good journey." I am yet again floored by the power of God and the power that is my angel Makenzie Goode. Thank you for continuing to spread her story. It will continue to make a difference and resonate with those of us who were her friends and needed her in our lives.

PVRS Crew Team named their vessel after Makenzie in 2010

About the Book Cover

I found this picture of Kenzie in among her thousands of pictures. It is one of very few where she is not smiling nor goofing off. I was told she took this selfie while riding the school bus and looking out the window. It certainly is contemplative. The background of the book cover is a sunrise that I snapped one early morning at the accident site. It's beauty just captivated me. I was sent so many ideas for book cover samples but none seemed right. On a whim (or a Godwink?) I decided to send the sunrise picture off to the graphic artist who was creating our book cover and she made magic with it! Like the book, the cover is to me, a piece of my heart created by daughter and mother.

CPSIA information can be obtained
at www.ICGtesting.com
Printed in the USA
BVHW010827251021
619809BV00024B/456